BASIS FOR BUSINESS

PHRASEBOOK

B1

BASIS FOR BUSINESS B1 Phrasebook

Im Auftrag des Verlages erarbeitet von	Zsuzsa Parádi
Redaktionelle Mitarbeit	Eva Schmidt
Redaktion	Anna Batrla
Projektleitung	Murdo MacPhail
Gesamtgestaltung und technische Umsetzung	Sabine Theuring, Berlin
Umschlagfoto	Mauritius images/Pixtal

www.cornelsen.de

1. Auflage, 1. Druck 2011

Alle Drucke dieser Auflage sind inhaltlich unverändert und können im Unterricht nebeneinander verwendet werden.

Druck: CS-Druck CornelsenStürtz, Berlin

ISBN 978-3-06-521005-8

 Inhalt gedruckt auf säurefreiem Papier aus nachhaltiger Forstwirtschaft.

Im **BASIS FOR BUSINESS B1 Phrasebook** können Sie die Wörter, die im Kursbuch vorkommen, in mehreren Vokabelverzeichnissen nachschlagen.

In der chronologischen Wortliste sind für jede englische Vokabel die deutsche Übersetzung sowie die Aussprache der Vokabel in phonetischer Umschrift angegeben.
Diese Wortliste enthält darüber hinaus Kästen, in denen wichtige Redewendungen thematisch für Sie zusammengefasst sind. So sehen Sie auf einen Blick, mit welchen sprachlichen Mitteln Sie sich in bestimmten geschäftlichen Situationen am besten ausdrücken können.
Die Reihenfolge der Wörter in der chronologischen Liste entspricht der Reihenfolge ihres Auftretens in den einzelnen Units. Als Orientierungshilfe sind die Wörter den einzelnen Teilen einer Unit (*Part A, Part B, Business file, Extra practice*) bzw. den Hörtexten zugeordnet. Die Information zur Fundstelle steht auch am jeweiligen Seitenende. Die *Exercise*-Nummern links neben den Wörtern helfen Ihnen dabei, das entsprechende Wort im Kursbuch schnell zu finden.

Darüber hinaus bietet das **BASIS FOR BUSINESS B1 Phrasebook** ein alphabetisches Register (Englisch-Deutsch) zum bequemen Nachschlagen einzelner Wörter sowie eine Liste zu Orten, Ländern und Nationalitäten.

Viel Spaß beim Lernen mir Ihrem **BASIS FOR BUSINESS B1 Phrasebook**!

Inhalt

Verwendete Abkürzungen

WU	Welcome unit	abbr.	abbreviation (Abkürzung)
BF	Business file	sth	something
GS	Grammar summary	sb	somebody
EP	Extra practice	jmd	jemand
BC	Business correspondence	jmdm	jemandem
coll.	colloquial (umgangssprachlich)	jmdn	jemanden
AmE	American English	jmds	jemandes
BrE	British English	etw	etwas

Verwendete Symbole

▶ warm-up exercise

◉ Hörtext

Hinweise zur Aussprache

ɑː wie in **a**sk [ɑːsk]

ʌ wie in n**u**mber ['nʌmbə]

æ wie in c**a**n [kæn]

e wie in **e**nter ['entə]

iː wie in h**e** [hiː]

i wie in happ**y** ['hæpi]

ɪ wie in s**i**t [sɪt]

ɜː wie in b**i**rthday ['bɜːθdeɪ]

ɒ wie in g**o**t [gɒt]

ɔː wie in f**ou**r [fɔː]

ʊ wie in b**oo**k [bʊk]

uː wie in f**oo**d [fuːd]

u wie in sit**u**ation [ˌsɪtʃu'eɪʃn]

ə wie in fath**er** ['fɑːðə]

aɪ wie in fl**i**ght ['flaɪt]

aʊ wie in **ou**t [aʊt]

eɪ wie in d**a**te [deɪt]

ɔɪ wie in b**oy** [bɔɪ]

ɪə wie in h**ear** [hɪə]

eə wie in h**air** [heə]

əʊ wie in ph**o**ne [fəʊn]

Welcome!

1	to go with sth	['gəʊ wɪθ]	zu etw passen
2	in person	[ɪn 'pɜːsn]	persönlich, selbst
	common	['kɒmən]	gemeinsam, allgemein
	to have sth in common with sb	[ɪn 'kɒmən]	etw mit jmdm gemeinsam haben
	hometown	['həʊmtaʊn]	Heimatort, Heimatstadt
	originally	[ə'rɪdʒənəli]	ursprünglich
	kind	[kaɪnd]	Art, Sorte
	what kind of	[wɒt 'kaɪnd əv]	was für, welche
3	face to face	[ˌfeɪs tə 'feɪs]	von Angesicht zu Angesicht
	to take part in sth	[teɪk 'pɑːt ɪn]	an etw teilnehmen
	teleconference	['telikɒnfərəns]	Konferenzschaltung, Telekonferenz
	trade	[treɪd]	Fach, Branche, Gewerbe, Handel
	journal	['dʒɜːnl]	Zeitung, Zeitschrift
	trade journal	['treɪd dʒɜːnl]	Fachzeitschrift, Handelsblatt
	business partner	['bɪznəs pɑːtnə]	Geschäftsparter/in
4	goal	[gəʊl]	Ziel
	be able to do sth	['eɪbl tə du]	etw tun können
5	character	['kærəktə]	Figur, Person
	clue	[kluː]	Hinweis, Tipp
	yogurt	['jɒgət]	Joghurt
	to come on the market	[kʌm ɒn ðə 'mɑːkɪt]	auf den Markt kommen
	medium-sized	['miːdiəm saɪzd]	mittelgroß
	dairy product	['deəri prɒdʌkt]	Milchprodukt
	to run a company	[ˌrʌn ə 'kʌmpəni]	ein Geschäft führen, betreiben
	to stock sth	[stɒk]	etw lagern, führen
	vending machine	['vendɪŋ məʃiːn]	(Verkaufs-)Automat
	to export	[ɪk'spɔːt]	exportieren
	all over	[ɒl 'əʊvə]	überall
	to clean	[kliːn]	putzen, säubern
	cleaning product	['kliːnɪŋ prɒdʌkt]	Putzmittel
	winery	['waɪnəri]	Weingut
6	to take turns	[teɪk 'tɜːns]	sich abwechseln
	native speaker	[ˌneɪtɪv 'spiːkə]	Muttersprachler/in
	non-native speaker	[nɒn ˌneɪtɪv 'spiːkə]	Nichtmuttersprachler/in
	subsidiary	[səb'sɪdieri]	Tochtergesellschaft
	located	[ləʊ'keɪtɪd]	gelegen

UNIT 1, Part A

impression	[ɪm'preʃn]	Eindruck
▶ to meet up with sb	[ˌmiːt 'ʌp wɪð]	sich mit jmdm treffen
alone	[ə'ləʊn]	allein
1 lab (informal: laboratory)	[læb, lə'bɒrətri]	Labor
supervisor	['suːpəvaɪzə]	Leiter/in
call centre	['kɔːl sentə]	Callcenter
agent	['eɪdʒənt]	hier: Bearbeiter/in, Mitarbeiter/in
safety engineer	['seɪfti endʒɪnɪə]	Sicherheitsingenieur/in, -techniker/in
production line	[prə'dʌkʃn laɪn]	Produktionsanlage, Fertigungslinie
reader	['riːdə]	Leser/in
east	[iːst]	ost-, östlich
kitchen	['kɪtʃɪn]	Küche
corridor	['kɒrɪdɔː]	Flur, Korridor
decaf (abbr.: decaffeinated)	[ˌdiː'kæf, ˌdiː'kæfɪneɪtɪd]	koffeinfrei
steady	['stedi]	fest, zuverlässig
chat	[tʃæt]	Plausch, kurze Unterhaltung
it's time to …	[ɪts 'taɪm]	es ist Zeit für / um …
microscope	['maɪkrəskəʊp]	Mikroskop
first thing	[fɜːst 'θɪŋ]	als erstes, gleich
refreshment	[rɪ'freʃmənt]	Erfrischung, Imbiss
pastry	['peɪstri]	Gebäck(stück)
to get started	[get 'stɑːtəd]	anfangen, loslegen
diary	['daɪəri]	(Termin-)Kalender
to get away	[get ə'weɪ]	wegkommen, weggehen
to have the phone on	[həv ðə 'fəʊn ɒn]	das Telefon eingeschaltet haben
deputy	['depjuti]	Stellvertreter/in
to take a break	[teɪk ə 'breɪk]	eine Pause machen
rotating	[rəʊ'teɪtɪŋ]	rotierend
basis	['beɪsɪs]	Basis
in fact	[ɪn 'fækt]	um genau zu sein, eigentlich
during	['djʊərɪŋ]	während
to spend time on sth	[spend 'taɪm ɒn]	Zeit verbringen mit etw

Having a coffee break

How often do you have a coffee break?	Wie oft machen Sie eine Kaffeepause?
We usually meet up at … o'clock.	Normalerweise treffen wir uns gegen … Uhr.
I meet up with … first thing in the morning.	Morgens treffe ich mich als Erstes mit …
It's time to get started.	Es ist Zeit, (mit der Arbeit) anzufangen.
I usually have quite an early break.	Ich mache normalerweise relativ früh Pause.

2	workday	['wɜːkdeɪ]	Arbeitstag
	to **get up**	[get 'ʌp]	aufstehen
	to **get to work**	[get tə 'wɜːk]	zur Arbeit gehen/kommen
3	related	[rɪ'leɪtɪd]	zusammenhängend
	payroll	['peɪrəʊl]	Gehaltsrechnung
	training	['treɪnɪŋ]	Ausbildung, Einarbeitung, Schulung
	focus	['fəʊkəs]	Fokus, Mittelpunkt
	to **move around**	[muːv ə'raʊnd]	umherbewegen, transportieren
	to **draw up**	[ˌdrɔː 'ʌp]	*hier:* entwerfen

Departments

HR = Human Ressources	Personalwesen
IT = Information Technology	Informationstechnolgie
R&D = Research and Development	Forschung und Entwicklung
Sales	Verkauf, Vertrieb
Legal	Rechtsabteilung
Purchasing	Einkauf
Logistics and Distribution	Logistik und Versand

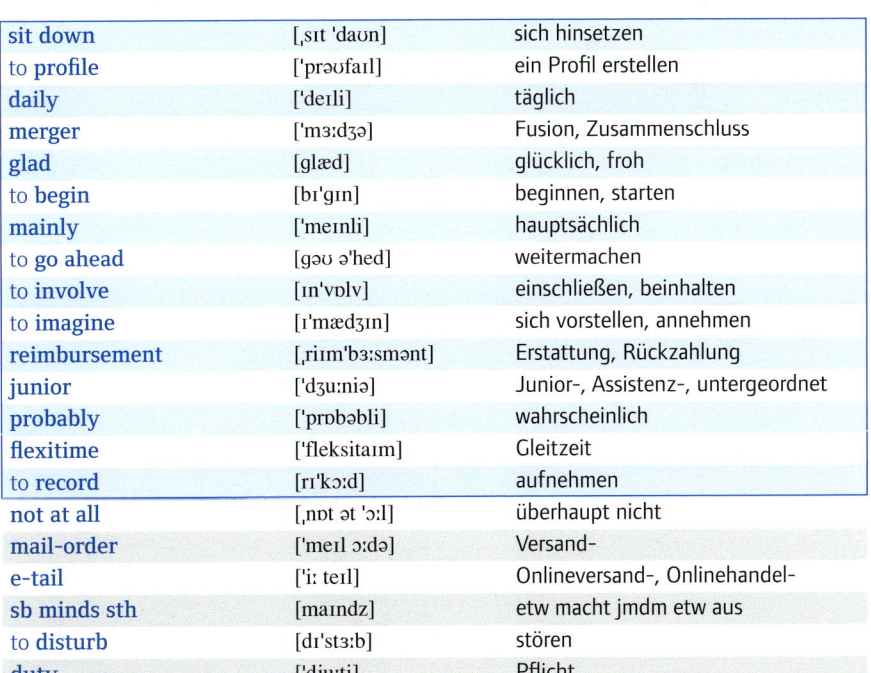

4	sit down	[ˌsɪt 'daʊn]	sich hinsetzen
1.2	to **profile**	['prəʊfaɪl]	ein Profil erstellen
	daily	['deɪli]	täglich
	merger	['mɜːdʒə]	Fusion, Zusammenschluss
	glad	[glæd]	glücklich, froh
	to **begin**	[bɪ'gɪn]	beginnen, starten
	mainly	['meɪnli]	hauptsächlich
	to **go ahead**	[gəʊ ə'hed]	weitermachen
	to **involve**	[ɪn'vɒlv]	einschließen, beinhalten
	to **imagine**	[ɪ'mædʒɪn]	sich vorstellen, annehmen
	reimbursement	[ˌriːm'bɜːsmənt]	Erstattung, Rückzahlung
	junior	['dʒuːniə]	Junior-, Assistenz-, untergeordnet
	probably	['prɒbəbli]	wahrscheinlich
	flexitime	['fleksitaɪm]	Gleitzeit
	to **record**	[rɪ'kɔːd]	aufnehmen
	not at all	[ˌnɒt ət 'ɔːl]	überhaupt nicht
	mail-order	['meɪl ɔːdə]	Versand-
	e-tail	['iː teɪl]	Onlineversand-, Onlinehandel-
	sb minds sth	[maɪndz]	etw macht jmdm etw aus
	to **disturb**	[dɪ'stɜːb]	stören
	duty	['djuːti]	Pflicht

It's …, isn't it?	Sie sind …, oder?
Are you …, by any chance?	Sind Sie zufällig …?
Do you mind if I ask you a question?	Darf ich Ihnen eine Frage stellen?
Do you have a moment?	Hätten Sie einen Moment Zeit?
I hope I'm not disturbing you.	Ich hoffe, ich störe Sie nicht.
Nice to meet you in person.	Schön, Sie persönlich kennenzulernen.
Is now a good time for you?	Wäre es Ihnen jetzt recht?

5	several	['sevrəl]	mehrere, einige
	collocation	[ˌkɒlə'keɪʃn]	Kollokation
	for a living	[fər ə 'lɪvɪŋ]	als Beruf, für den Lebensunterhalt
7	retail	['riːteɪl]	Einzelhandel
1.3	fashion	['fæʃn]	Mode
	furniture	['fɜːnɪtʃə]	Möbel
	mail order	[ˌmeɪl 'ɔːdə]	Versandhandel
	immediate	[ɪ'miːdiət]	unmittelbar, sofort
	to report to sb	[rɪ'pɔːt tə]	jmdm unterstellt sein
	closely	['kləʊsli]	eng, dicht
	supervisor	['suːpəvaɪzə]	Leiter/in
	directly	[də'rektli]	direkt, unmittelbar
	support	[sə'pɔːt]	Unterstützung
	to (give) support	[gɪv sə'pɔːt]	unterstützen
	to head sth up	[hed 'ʌp]	etw leiten
	care	[keə]	Sorge, Betreuung
	customer care	[ˌkʌstəmə 'keə]	Kundendienst, Kundenbetreuung
	purely	['pjʊəli]	rein
	social	['səʊʃl]	privat, sozial, gesellschaftlich
	to supervise	['suːpəvaɪz]	betreuen, leiten, überwachen
	head	[hed]	Leiter/in

Responsibilities and roles I

She's in sales.	Sie arbeitet in der Vertriebsabteilung.
I update / deal with / handle / coordinate ...	Ich aktualisiere / bearbeite / habe mit ... zu tun / koordiniere ...
She has five direct reports.	Sie ist direkte Vorgesetzte von fünf Mitarbeitern/ Mitarbeiterinnen.
I'm mainly responsible for ...	Ich bin hauptsächlich für ... verantwortlich.
My immediate boss is ...	Meine direkte Vorgesetzte / mein direkter Vorgesetzter ist ...
I work closely with ...	Ich arbeite eng mit ... zusammen.
Mark reports directly to ...	Mark ist ... unmittelbar unterstellt.
... heads up the team.	... leitet das Team.
I have lots of nice colleagues in several other departments, too.	Ich habe auch viele nette Kolleginnen/Kollegen in verschiedenen anderen Abteilungen.
I sometimes meet up with ... on a purely social basis.	Ich treffe ... manchmal rein privat.

8	either ... or ...	[ˌaɪðər ˈɔː]	entweder ... oder ...
	junior manager	[ˌdʒuːniə ˈmænɪdʒə]	Nachwuchsführungskraft
	direct report	[dəˌrəkt rɪˈpɔːt]	unmittelbar Unterstellte/r
	to input	[ˈɪnpʊt]	eingeben
	clerk	[klɑːk]	Büroangestellte/r
	to summarize	[ˈsʌməraɪz]	zusammenfassen
	to read out	[ˌriːd ˈaʊt]	vorlesen
	graphic	[ˈgræfɪk]	Grafik
	senior	[ˈsiːniə]	leitend
	trainee	[ˌtreɪˈniː]	Auszubildende/r, Trainee
9	to spot	[spɒt]	entdecken
	lie	[laɪ]	Lüge
	oil	[ɔɪl]	Öl
	civil	[ˈsɪvl]	Bürger-, Staats-
	civil service	[ˌsɪvl ˈsɜːvɪs]	Behörde, öffentlicher Dienst
	to be between jobs	[bɪtwiːn ˈdʒɒbs]	arbeitslos sein
	opening	[ˈəʊpnɪŋ]	hier: freie Stelle
	dentist	[ˈdentɪst]	Zahnarzt, Zahnärztin
	hospital	[ˈhɒspɪtl]	Krankenhaus

UNIT 1, Part B

▶ corporate culture	[ˌkɔːpərət ˈkʌltʃə]	Unternehmenskultur
1 sitemap	[ˈsaɪtmæp]	Seitenübersicht, Strukturkarte
E-Business	[ˈiː bɪznəs]	Internetgeschäft, -firma
innovation	[ˌɪnəˈveɪʃn]	Neuerung, Innovation
sustainability	[səˌsteɪnəˈbɪləti]	Nachhaltigkeit, Umweltschutz
business unit	[ˈbɪznəs juːnɪt]	Geschäftsbereich
vision	[ˈvɪʒn]	Vision
adhesive	[ədˈhiːsɪv]	Klebstoff
vibrant	[ˈvaɪbrənt]	dynamisch
industrial	[ɪnˈdʌstriəl]	industriell, Industrie-
glue	[gluː]	Klebstoff, Leim
diverse	[daɪˈvɜːs]	unterschiedlich, vielfältig
aeroplane	[ˈeərəpleɪn]	Flugzeug
nappy	[ˈnæpi]	Windel
continent	[ˈkɒntɪnənt]	Kontinent
region	[ˈriːdʒən]	Region, Gebiet, Gegend
throughout	[θruːˈaʊt]	überall
to set	[set]	setzen, stellen, legen
business activity	[ˈbɪznəs æktɪvəti]	Geschäftsaktivität
divided	[dɪˈvaɪdəd]	aufgeteilt
automotive	[ˌɔːtəˈməʊtɪv]	Automobil-, Kraftfahrzeug-
aeronautics	[ˌeərəˈnɔːtɪks]	Flugtechnik
hygiene	[ˈhaɪdʒiːn]	Hygiene
division	[dɪˈvɪʒn]	Abteilung
2 organization	[ˌɔːrgənəˈzeɪʃn]	Organisation, Unternehmen, Einteilung
flat	[flæt]	flach
basically	[ˈbeɪsɪkli]	im Grunde, im Prinzip
layer	[ˈleɪə]	Schicht, Ebene
top	[tɒp]	Spitze
senior manager	[ˌsiːniə ˈmænɪdʒə]	Abteilungsleiter/in
various	[ˈveəriəs]	verschiedene
rest	[rest]	Rest
parent company	[ˈpeərənt kʌmpəni]	Muttergesellschaft

Corporate organizations

Ltd. = Limited Company (BrE)	(in etwa) GmbH
plc = Public Limited Company (BrE)	(in etwa) AG
Inc./Corp. = Incorporated Closed	
Corporation (AmE)	(in etwa) GmbH
Open Corporation (AmE)	(in etwa) AG
CEO = Chief Executive Officer	Vorstandschef/in, Geschäftsführer/in
CFO = Chief Financial Officer	Finanzvorstand, Finanzchef/in, Leiter/in
	der Finanzabteilung
CIO = Chief Information Officer	Leiter/in der Abteilung Informationstechnologie
COO = Chief Operating Officer	Betriebsleiter/in
CRO = Chief Risk Officer	Risikomanager/in
CTO = Chief Technology Officer	Technische Direktorin/Technischer Direktor

4
1.4

trusted	['trʌstəd]	zuverlässig, vertraut
brand name	['brænd neɪm]	Markenname
to specialize (in sth)	['speʃəlaɪz]	sich (auf etw) spezialisieren
hair-care	['heə keə]	Haarpflege
body	['bɒdi]	Körper
soap	[səʊp]	Seife
bath	[bɑːθ]	Bad
according to	[ə'kɔːdɪŋ tə]	zufolge, laut, nach, entsprechend
customer base	['kʌstəmə beɪs]	Kundenstamm, Kundschaft
obviously	['ɒbviəsli]	natürlich, selbstverständlich
level	['levl]	Niveau, Grad
to teach	[tiːtʃ]	lehren

1.5

utility	[juː'tɪləti]	Nutzen, *hier:* Versorgungsbetrieb
utility company	[juː'tɪləti kʌmpəni]	Elektrizitätswerk, Energieversorger
plant	[plɑːnt]	Fabrik, Werk, Maschinen
to meet a standard	[miːt ə 'stændəd]	eine Norm erfüllen, einem Standard entsprechen
pyramid	['pɪrəmɪd]	Pyramide
bottom	['bɒtəm]	Grund, Boden
workforce	['wɜːkfɔːs]	Belegschaft, Arbeitskräfte
especially	[ɪ'speʃəli]	besonders, vor allem
habit	['hæbɪt]	Gewohnheit, Angewohnheit
work habits	['wɜːk hæbɪts]	Arbeitseinstellung
on a regular basis	[ɒn ə ˌregjələ 'beɪsɪs]	regelmäßig
to generate	['dʒenəreɪt]	erzeugen
hydroelectric	[ˌhaɪdrəʊɪ'lektrɪk]	hydroelektrisch
power	['paʊə]	*hier:* Strom, Energie

to construct	[kənˈstrʌkt]	bauen, errichten
station	[ˈsteɪʃn]	Station
hydroelectric power station	[haɪdrəʊˌlektrɪk ˈpaʊə steɪʃn]	Wasserkraftwerk
careers fair	[kəˈrɪəz feə]	Firmenmesse, Jobbörse
straightforward	[ˌstreɪtˈfɔːwəd]	einfach
environmentally-friendly	[ɪnvaɪrənˌmentəli ˈfrendli]	umweltfreundlich
to grow	[grəʊ]	wachsen, zunehmen, steigen
long-established	[lɒŋ ɪˈstæblɪʃt]	alteingeführt, alteingesessen

Company structure

The company structure is quite flat.	Die Struktur in der Firma ist relativ flach.
It's basically divided into three layers.	Sie ist im Prinzip in drei Ebenen unterteilt.
… is at the top.	… steht an der Spitze.
… are in the second layer.	… sind auf der mittleren Ebene.
Our structure is very traditional.	Unsere Struktur ist sehr traditionell.
There is a parent company.	Es gibt eine Muttergesellschaft.
The subsidiaries are operating in different regions.	Die Tochtergesellschaften sind in verschiedenen Regionen tätig.

5	familiar with sth	[fəˈmɪliə wɪð]	mit etw vertraut
6	to target	[ˈtɑːgɪt]	zielen auf
	surprisingly	[səˈpraɪzɪŋliː]	überraschenderweise
	garment	[ˈgɑːmənt]	Kleidungsstück
	to wonder	[ˈwʌndə]	sich fragen
	premium	[ˈpriːmiəm]	erstklassig, Spitzen-
	fresh	[freʃ]	frisch
	natural	[ˈnætʃrəl]	natürlich, Natur-
	ingredient	[ɪnˈgriːdɪənt]	Zutat
	Alpine	[ˈælpaɪn]	Alpen-, alpin
	vanilla	[vəˈnɪlə]	Vanille
7	to guess	[ges]	raten, schätzen, erraten
	beyond	[bɪˈjɒnd]	darüber hinaus
	space	[speɪs]	Raum
	gummi bear	[ˈgʌmi beə]	Gummibärchen
	hand cream	[ˈhænd kriːm]	Handcreme
	sandal	[ˈsændl]	Sandale
	figure	[ˈfɪgə]	Figur

UNIT 1, Business file

1	vintage	['vɪntɪdʒ]	alt, altmodisch, klassisch
1.6	vintage car	['vɪntɪdʒ kɑː]	Oldtimer
	rental	['rentl]	Verleih
	full	[fʊl]	vollständig
	to return a call	[rɪːtɜːn ə 'kɒl]	zurückrufen
1.7	would love	[wʊd 'lʌv]	hätte(n) gern, würde(n) gern
	otherwise	['ʌðəwaɪz]	sonst, ansonsten
1.8	to catch up	[kætʃ 'ʌp]	*hier:* treffen
2	last name	['lɑːst neɪm]	Nachname
	first name	['fɜːst neɪm]	Vorname
	to catch	[kætʃ]	*hier:* verstehen, mitbekommen
	to read back	[riːd 'bæk]	nochmal vorlesen, wiederholen

Passing on and checking contact details

I'm sorry, I didn't catch that.	Entschuldigung, das habe ich nicht verstanden.
What's your last name again?	Wie war doch gleich Ihr Nachname?
How do you spell that, please?	Wie schreibt man das, bitte?
Could you please say that again/ repeat that?	Könnten Sie das bitte noch einmal sagen/ wiederholen?
Can I read that back?	Kann ich das wiederholen?
Sorry, is this spelled with a double 'g'?	Entschuldigung, schreibt man das mit zwei 'g'?

3	unique	[juˈniːk]	einzigartig, einmalig
1.9	vehicle	['viːəkl]	Fahrzeug
	to hire	['haɪə]	mieten, leihen
	limousine	['lɪməziːn]	Limousine, Straßenkreuzer
	old-fashioned	[ˌəʊld 'fæʃnd]	altmodisch
	farm	[fɑːm]	Bauernhof, Farm
	tractor	['træktə]	Traktor
	treat	[triːt]	Vergnügen, Genuss, etwas Besonderes
	commercial	[kəˈmɜːʃl]	Werbespot
	fun	[fʌn]	Spaß
	to get to do (sth)	[get tə 'duː]	die Möglichkeit haben, etw zu tun
	film star	['fɪlm stɑː]	Filmstar
1.10	to found	[faʊnd]	gründen
	Chardonnay	['ʃɑːdəneɪ]	Chardonnay
	loyal	['lɔɪəl]	treu, loyal
	speedy	['spiːdi]	schnell
	for one thing	[fər 'wʌn θɪŋ]	zum einen

	delicious	[dɪˈlɪʃəs]	köstlich
	art	[ɑːt]	Kunst
	museum	[mjuˈziːəm]	Museum
◉)1.11	community bank	[kəˈmjuːnəti bæŋk]	lokale/unabhängige Bank
	poor	[pɔː]	arm, armselig
	village	[ˈvɪlɪdʒ]	Dorf
	to start up	[stɑːt ˈʌp]	gründen
	to lend	[lend]	leihen
	to inspire	[ɪnˈspaɪə]	inspirieren, anspornen
4	to stand out	[stænd ˈaʊt]	auffallen, hervorstechen
	crowd	[kraʊd]	Menge, Masse
	these days	[ˈðiːz deɪz]	heutzutage
	to reach out	[riːtʃ ˈaʊt]	*hier:* seine Fühler ausstrecken
	professionals	[prəˈfeʃənls]	Fachleute
	similar	[ˈsɪmələ]	ähnlich
	completely	[kəmˈpliːtlɪ]	völlig, absolut, total
	field	[fiːld]	Gebiet, Feld
	memorable	[ˈmemərəbl]	unvergesslich, einprägsam
	factor	[ˈfæktə]	Faktor
	to choose	[tʃuːz]	wählen
	concrete	[ˈkɒŋkriːt]	konkret
	home delivery	[ˌhəʊm dɪˈlɪvəriː]	Hauszustellung
	specific	[spəˈsɪfɪk]	präzise, spezifisch
	to serve	[sɜːv]	bedienen
	estate	[ɪˈsteɪt]	Besitz, Wohnsiedlung, (Land-)Gut
	estate agency	[ɪˈsteɪt eɪdʒənsi]	Immobilienbüro
	cupcake	[ˈkʌpkeɪk]	kleiner Rührkuchen
	home-made	[ˌhəʊm ˈmeɪd]	selbstgemacht
	to decorate	[ˈdekəreɪt]	dekorieren, schmücken, verzieren
	by hand	[baɪ ˈhænd]	in Handarbeit
	to crunch	[krʌntʃ]	*hier:* verarbeiten
	number-cruncher	[ˈnʌmbə krʌntʃə]	jmd, der gut mit Zahlen umgehen kann
5	self	[self]	selbst
	second	[ˈsekənd]	Sekunde
	rather	[ˈrɑːðə]	ziemlich

UNIT 1, Extra practice

1	sugar	[ˈʃʊgə]	Zucker
	noon	[nuːn]	Mittag
2	to expand	[ɪkˈspænd]	expandieren, vergrößern
3	rearrange	[ˌriːəˈreɪndʒ]	umstellen, ändern

5	drug record	[ˌdrʌg ˈrekɔːd]	Medikamentenregister/-verzeichnis
	wages	[ˈweɪdʒəs]	Lohn
	pharmaceutical	[ˌfɑːməˈsuːtɪkl]	pharmazeutisch
6	slowly	[ˈsləʊli]	langsam
	multinational	[ˌmʌltiˈnæʃnəl]	multinational
	manufacturer	[ˌmænjuˈfæktʃərə]	Hersteller
CS	tricky	[ˈtrɪki]	schwierig, verzwickt
	harmless	[ˈhɑːmləs]	harmlos
	to react	[riˈækt]	reagieren
	light-hearted	[ˌlaɪt ˈhɑːtəd]	unbeschwert
	enough	[iˈnʌf]	genug
	to get by	[get ˈbaɪ]	zurechtkommen
	particular	[pəˈtɪkjələ]	bestimmt, speziell, besondere/r/s
	in particular	[ɪn pəˈtɪkjələ]	vor allem, ganz besonders
	understatement	[ˌʌndəˈsteɪtmənt]	Untertreibung, Understatement
	to connect with sb	[kəˈnekt wɪð]	mit jmdm in Verbindung treten
	impolite	[ˌɪmpəˈlaɪt]	unhöflich
	advice	[ədˈvaɪs]	Ratschlag
	lead	[liːd]	Beispiel, Anhaltspunkt
	doubt	[daʊt]	Zweifel, Ungewissheit
	to specify	[ˈspesɪfaɪ]	angeben
	hierarchy	[ˈhaɪərɑːki]	Hierarchie
	gentle	[ˈdʒentl]	vorsichtig

UNIT 2, Part A

	then	[ðen]	damals
	past	[pɑːst]	Vergangenheit
	ability	[əˈbɪləti]	Fähigkeit
1	syllable	[ˈsɪləbl]	Silbe
1.13	to stress	[stres]	betonen
	column	[ˈkɒləm]	Spalte
	component	[kəmˈpəʊnənt]	Bestandteil, Komponente
	bureaucracy	[bjʊəˈrɒkrəsi]	Bürokratie
	opportunity	[ˌɒpəˈtjuːnəti]	Gelegenheit
	importance	[ɪmˈpɔːtns]	Wichtigkeit, Bedeutung
	meaning	[ˈmiːnɪŋ]	Bedeutung
	producer	[prəˈdjuːsə]	Hersteller
	official	[əˈfɪʃl]	offiziell
	chance	[tʃɑːns]	Gelegenheit, Chance
2	to meet	[miːt]	*hier:* erfüllen
	mechanical	[mɪˈkænɪkl]	maschinell, Maschinen-
	to graduate	[ˈgrædʒueɪt]	einen Abschluss machen

	to **be behind schedule**	[bɪ,haɪnd 'ʃedjuːl]	im Verzug sein
	to **switch**	[swɪtʃ]	tauschen, wechseln
	hectic	['hektɪk]	hektisch
	rapid	['ræpɪd]	schnell
	combination	[,kɒmbɪ'neɪʃn]	Kombination, Verbindung
	former	['fɔːmə]	früher, ehemalig
	benefit	['benɪfɪt]	Nutzen, Vorteil
	mix	[mɪks]	Mischung, Mix
4	**professional**	[prə'feʃənl]	beruflich
5	**outskirts**	['aʊtskɜːts]	Stadtrand, Außenbezirke
1.14	**economical**	[,iːkə'nɒmɪkl]	sparsam
	few	[fjuː]	wenige
	temporary	['temprəri]	befristet, vorübergehend
	security	[sɪ'kjʊərəti]	Sicherheit
	prompt	[prɒmpt]	Stichwort
	used to do sth	[juːst tə 'duː]	früher etw getan haben
7	to **invite**	[ɪn'vaɪt]	einladen
	need	[niːd]	Bedürfnis
	context	['kɒntekst]	Zusammenhang, Kontext
	skiing	['skiːɪŋ]	Skifahren
	cycling	['saɪklɪŋ]	Radfahren
	driven	['drɪvn]	angetrieben
8	**résumé** (AmE)	['rezjumeɪ]	Lebenslauf
	association	[ə,səʊsi'eɪʃn]	Kontakt, Verband
	sex	[seks]	Geschlecht
	educational	[,edʒu'keɪʃənl]	Lern-, Ausbildungs-, Bildungs-
	academic	[,ækə'demɪk]	Schul-, wissenschaftlich, akademisch
	background	['bækgraʊnd]	Hintergrund
	ethnic	['eθnɪk]	ethnisch
	maternity	[mə'tɜːnəti]	Mutterschaft
	paternity	[pə'tɜːnəti]	Vaterschaft
	leave	[liːv]	Urlaub
	complete	[kəm'pliːt]	komplett, vollständig
	history	['hɪstri]	Geschichte, Vorgeschichte
	marital	['mærɪtl]	ehelich, Ehe-
	status	['steɪtəs]	Status, Stand
	relevant	['reləvənt]	relevant, einschlägig

Old job, new job

I'm between jobs.	Ich bin zurzeit arbeitslos.
I feel that I'm ready for more.	*(in etwa:)* Ich bin bereit für mehr Verantwortung/ größere Herausforderungen.
I'm looking for a new opening.	Ich suche nach einer neuen Stelle.
I switched to a start-up.	Ich bin zu einem Start-up-Unternehmen gewechselt.
I have my own office now but I didn't use to before.	Ich habe jetzt mein eigenes Büro, aber das war nicht immer so.

UNIT 2, Part B

1	internal	[ɪnˈtɜːnl]	intern
	to **optimize**	[ˈɒptɪmaɪz]	optimieren
	to **integrate**	[ˈɪntɪɡreɪt]	integrieren, sich eingliedern
	expertise	[ˌekspɜːˈtiːz]	Fachwissen, Sachverstand
	to **come your way**	[kʌm jɔː ˈweɪ]	einem über den Weg laufen
	understaffed	[ˌʌndəˈstɑːft]	unterbesetzt
	challenge	[ˈtʃælɪndʒ]	Herausforderung
	to **delegate**	[ˈdelɪɡeɪt]	delegieren, beauftragen
	council	[ˈkaʊnsl]	Rat
	works council	[ˌwɜːks ˈkaʊnsl]	Betriebsrat
2	to **expect**	[ɪkˈspekt]	erwarten
	pros and cons	[ˌprəʊz ən ˈkɒnz]	Pro und Contra

Responsibilities and roles II

I can delegate tasks.	Ich kann Aufgaben delegieren.
I can manage projects.	Ich kann Projekte leiten.
I can meet deadlines.	Ich kann Fristen/Termine einhalten.
I'm responsible for …	Ich bin verantwortlich für …
I can deal with everything that comes my way.	Ich kann mit allen möglichen Problemen umgehen.
In my last job, I was able to …	Während meiner letzten Tätigkeit konnte ich …
I used to be responsible for …	Ich war für … verantwortlich.
When I first started, I couldn't …, but now I can …	Als ich anfing, konnte ich nicht …, aber jetzt kann ich …
I am the specialist for …	Ich bin der/die Spezialist/in für …

4	hot-desking	[ˌhɒt ˈdeskɪŋ]	Arbeitsplatzwahl nach Verfügbarkeit
	furnished	[ˈfɜːnɪʃt]	eingerichtet, ausgestattet
	accommodation	[əˌkɒməˈdeɪʃn]	Unterkunft, Zimmer
	pleasant	[ˈpleznt]	angenehm

to encourage	[ɪnˈkʌrɪdʒ]	fördern
core	[kɔː]	Kern
bonus	[ˈbəʊnəs]	Bonus, Prämie
5 to publish	[ˈpʌblɪʃ]	veröffentlichen
survey	[ˈsɜːveɪ]	Überblick
e-book	[ˈiː bʊk]	elektronisches Buch
while	[waɪl]	während
to hold	[həʊld]	halten
actual	[ˈæktʃuəl]	wirklich
a couple of	[ˈkʌpl]	einige, (ein) paar
popularity	[ˌpɒpjuˈlærəti]	Popularität, Beliebtheit
to undergo	[ˌʌndəˈgəʊ]	sich unterziehen
solid	[ˈsɒlɪd]	fest
to persuade	[pəˈsweɪd]	überreden, überzeugen
mind	[maɪnd]	Verstand, Gedanken
wholesale	[ˈhəʊlseɪl]	Großhandels-
revenue	[ˈrevənjuː]	Einkünfte, Einnahmen
recognition	[ˌrekəgˈnɪʃn]	Anerkennung
dramatically	[drəˈmætɪkli]	dramatisch
indication	[ˌɪndɪˈkeɪʃn]	Anzeichen, Hinweis
7 generation	[ˌdʒenəˈreɪʃn]	Generation
to criticize	[ˈkrɪtɪsaɪz]	kritisieren
to release	[rɪˈliːs]	veröffentlichen, herausbringen
to download	[ˌdaʊnˈləʊd]	herunterladen
wireless	[ˈwaɪələs]	kabellos

UNIT 2, Business file

1 pretty	[ˈprɪti]	ziemlich
1.16 say ...	[seɪ]	*hier:* zum Beispiel ...
cut off	[ˌkʌt ˈɒf]	*hier:* unterbrochen
to return	[rɪˈtɜːn]	zurückkommen
2 honest	[ˈɒnɪst]	ehrlich
1.17 accordingly	[əˈkɔːdɪŋli]	dementsprechend, folglich
3 to promise	[ˈprɒmɪs]	versprechen
caller	[ˈkɔːlə]	Anrufer/in
to end	[end]	beenden
5 to invent	[ɪnˈvent]	erfinden, sich ausdenken
unacceptable	[ˌʌnəkˈseptəbl]	nicht akzeptabel

UNIT 2, Extra practice

1	to rewrite	[ˌriːˈraɪt]	umschreiben
4	nowadays	[ˈnaʊədeɪz]	heutzutage
5	yearly	[ˈjɪəli]	jährlich
6	haves	[hævs]	Besitz, die Habe
	want	[wɒnt]	Wunsch, Bedürfnis
	painting	[ˈpeɪntɪŋ]	Malerei, Malen
8	to ring	[rɪŋ]	klingeln
1.18	notebook	[ˈnəʊtbʊk]	Notizbuch
	echo	[ˈekəʊ]	Echo
	to upgrade	[ˌʌpˈgreɪd]	hier: aufrüsten
CS	cultural	[ˈkʌltʃərəl]	kulturell
	norm	[nɔːm]	Norm, Regel
	illegal	[ɪˈliːgl]	illegal
	employer	[ɪmˈplɔɪə]	Arbeitgeber/in
	personal	[ˈpɜːsənl]	persönlich, privat
	discrimination	[dɪˌskrɪmɪˈneɪʃn]	Diskriminierung
	law	[lɔː]	Gesetz, Recht
	unsuccessful	[ˌʌnsəkˈsesfl]	erfolglos
	applicant	[ˈæplɪkənt]	Bewerber/in
	to accuse	[əˈkjuːz]	anklagen
	final	[ˈfaɪnl]	letzte/r/s
	upon request	[əˌpɒn rɪˈkwest]	auf Nachfrage
	potential	[pəˈtenʃl]	potentiell
	to request sth	[rɪˈkwest]	um etw bitten
	procedure	[prəˈsiːdʒə]	Vorgehen, Verfahren
	to save	[seɪf]	sparen
	to send sth in	[ˌsend ˈɪn]	etw einschicken
	to consider	[kənˈsɪdə]	halten für, ansehen als
	usual	[ˈjuːʒuəl]	üblich, normal
	appropriate	[əˈprəʊpriət]	angemessen, passend, geeignet

UNIT 3, Part A

1	regulation	[ˌregjuˈleɪʃn]	Vorschrift, Bestimmung
	process	[ˈprəʊses]	Prozess
	footwear	[ˈfʊtweə]	Schuhwerk
	favour	[ˈfeɪvə]	Gefallen
	header	[ˈhedə]	Kopfzeile
	closing	[ˈkləʊzɪŋ]	Schluss
	introductory	[ˌɪntrəˈdʌktəri]	einleitend, einführend
	remark	[rɪˈmɑːk]	Bemerkung
	translation	[trænsˈleɪʃn]	Übersetzung
	sub	[sʌb]	Unter-
	contractor	[kənˈtræktə]	Vertragspartner/in
	pick-up	[ˈpɪkʌp]	Abholung
	urgently	[ˈɜːdʒəntli]	dringend
	ad (abbr.: advertisement)	[æd, ədˈvɜːtɪsmənt]	Anzeige
	to help out	[help ˈaʊt]	aushelfen
3	to wear	[weə]	*Kleidung:* tragen
4	production site	[prəˈdʌkʃn saɪt]	Fertigungsstätte
🔊 1.19	smoothly	[ˈsmuːðli]	reibungslos, problemlos
	suitcase	[ˈsuːtkeɪs]	Koffer
	whereabouts	[ˌweərəˈbaʊts]	*hier:* wo
6	beige	[beɪʒ]	beige
	arrow	[ˈærəʊ]	Pfeil
	biscuit	[ˈbɪskɪt]	Keks

Welcoming a visitor

You must be …	Sie müssen … sein.
Did you have a good trip?	Hatten Sie eine angenehme Reise?
I'd like you to meet …	Darf ich Ihnen … vorstellen.
May I introduce …?	Darf ich … vorstellen?
Can I take your coat/bag?	Kann ich Ihnen den Mantel / die Tasche abnehmen?
Can I get you something to drink?	Kann ich Ihnen etwas zu trinken bringen?
So, what's your first impression of …?	Also, wie ist Ihr erster Eindruck von …?

7	definition	[ˌdefɪˈnɪʃn]	Definition
	sabbatical	[səˈbætɪkl]	Forschungsurlaub, Sabbatjahr
	percentage	[pəˈsentɪdʒ]	Prozentsatz, Anteil
	commuter	[kəˈmjuːtə]	Pendler/in
	use	[juːz]	Gebrauch, Einsatz
	health	[helθ]	Gesundheit

	agricultural	[ˌægrɪˈkʌltʃərəl]	landwirtschaftlich
	to **adapt**	[əˈdæpt]	anpassen
	to **lose**	[luːz]	verlieren
	to **figure out**	[ˌfɪɡər ˈaʊt]	herausbekommen, ausrechnen
	highland	[ˈhaɪlænd]	Hochland
	shoemaker	[ˈʃuːmeɪkə]	Schuhmacher/in
	simple	[ˈsɪmpl]	einfach
	elegant	[ˈelɪɡənt]	elegant
	leather	[ˈleðə]	Leder
	terrain	[təˈreɪn]	Gelände, Terrain
	sturdy	[ˈstɜːdi]	robust, stabil
	to **cycle**	[ˈsaɪkl]	Rad fahren
	smart	[smɑːt]	schick, fein
8	**half**	[hɑːf]	Hälfte
	tense	[tens]	Zeit
	action	[ˈækʃn]	Handlung
	one-time	[ˈwʌn taɪm]	einmalig

UNIT 3, Part B

◐	**drill**	[drɪl]	Übung
1	**welcome package**	[ˈwelkʌm pækɪdʒ]	Willkommens-Paket
	to **access**	[ˈækses]	erreichen
	protective	[prəˈtektɪv]	Schutz-, schützend
	headgear	[ˈhedɡɪə]	Kopfbedeckung
	earplug	[ˈɪəplʌg]	Ohrstöpsel
	to **smoke**	[sməʊk]	rauchen
	strictly	[ˈstrɪktli]	streng
	to **forbid**	[fəˈbɪd]	verbieten, untersagen
	premise	[ˈpremɪs]	Prämisse, Voraussetzung
	on the premises	[ɒn ðə ˈpremɪsəs]	im Hause
	designated	[ˈdezɪɡneɪtɪd]	gekennzeichnet
	minimum	[ˈmɪnɪməm]	Mindest-
	machinery	[məˈʃiːnəri]	Maschinerie, System
	to **mark**	[mɑːk]	markieren
	to **touch**	[tʌtʃ]	berühren
	to **attempt**	[əˈtempt]	versuchen
	close	[kləʊz]	dicht, nah
	instruction	[ɪnˈstrʌkʃn]	Anweisung
	to **head for**	[ˈhed fə]	(in eine Richtung) gehen
	exit	[ˈeksɪt]	Ausgang
	guideline	[ˈɡaɪdlaɪn]	Richtlinie
	switch	[swɪtʃ]	Schalter

2	leaflet	['li:flət]	Informationsblatt, Handzettel
	recommendation	[ˌrekəmen'deɪʃn]	Empfehlung
	emergency	[ɪ'mɜ:dʒənsi]	Notfall
3	shoemaking	['ʃu:meɪkɪŋ]	Schuhmacherei, -fabrikation
1.20	synthetic	[sɪn'θetɪk]	synthetisch
	to unload	[ˌʌn'ləʊd]	abladen, entladen
	shape	[ʃeɪp]	Form
	to cut out	[kʌt 'aʊt]	ausschneiden
	manually	['mænjuəli]	von Hand, manuell
	skilled	[skɪld]	Fach-, geschickt, ausgebildet
	pattern	['pætn]	Muster, Vorlage
	tool	[tu:l]	Werkzeug
	hand tool	['hænd tu:l]	Handwerkzeug
	upper	['ʌpə]	obere/r/s
	to sew	[səʊ]	nähen
	to attach	[ə'tætʃ]	befestigen
	sole	[səʊl]	Sohle
	finish	['fɪnɪʃ]	letzter Schliff, Finish
	to inspect	[ɪn'spekt]	überprüfen, kontrollieren
	defect	[dɪ'fekt]	Fehler, Defekt
	to wrap up	[ˌræp 'ʌp]	einpacken
	so to speak	[ˌsəʊ tə 'spi:k]	sozusagen
	indeed	[ɪn'di:d]	gewiss
	conveyor belt	[kən'veɪə belt]	Fließband, Förderband
	assembly line	[ə'sembli laɪn]	Montageband
5	thoroughly	['θʌrəli]	gründlich
	to unpack	[ˌʌn'pæk]	auspacken
	to remove	[rɪ'mu:v]	(weg-)transportieren
	damaged	['dæmɪdʒd]	beschädigt

Talking about processes

First / First of all …	Zunächst …
Next …	Als nächstes …
During this stage …	In diesem Stadium / In dieser Phase …
After that / Following that, …	Danach/Nachdem …
Finally …	Schließlich …
This is a very important stage.	Das ist eine sehr wichtige Phase.
It's quite a tricky/complicated process.	Das ist ein ziemlich verzwickter/komplizierter Prozess.

6	stationary	['steɪʃənri]	gleichbleibend
7	grateful	['greɪtfl]	dankbar
	recent	['riːsnt]	jüngst, aktuell
	stroll	[strəʊl]	Spaziergang, Bummel
	to taste	[teɪst]	schmecken
	gate	[geɪt]	Flugsteig
	to catch	[kætʃ]	erwischen, erreichen
	high heels	[ˌhaɪ 'hiːlz]	Schuhe mit hohen Absätzen
	to appreciate	[ə'priːʃieɪt]	dankbar sein

UNIT 3, Business file

1	interval	['ɪntəvl]	Pause
2	merchandise	['mɜːtʃəndaɪs]	Ware(n)
1.21	by chance	[baɪ 'tʃɑːns]	zufällig
	delighted	[dɪ'laɪtɪd]	erfreut, entzückt
	frequently	['friːkwəntli]	regelmäßig
	fabulous	['fæbjələs]	fabelhaft
	wheel	[wiːl]	Rad
1.22	Location Sourcing Manager	[ləʊ'keɪʃn sɔːsɪŋ mænɪdʒə]	Leiter/in der Abteilung für Standortsuche
	thrilled	[θrɪld]	begeistert, sehr froh
	mint	[mɪnt]	Minze, Pfefferminze
	speciality	[ˌspeʃi'æləti]	Spezialität
	district	['dɪstrɪkt]	Bezirk, Gebiet, Viertel
	energy bar	['enədʒi bɒː]	Energie-Riegel
	minty	['mɪnti]	Pfefferminz-, minzig
1.23	landscape	['lændskeɪp]	Landschaft
	impressive	[ɪm'presɪv]	beeindruckend
	to hike	[haɪk]	wandern
	trek	[trek]	Marsch, Treck
	to limit	['lɪmɪt]	begrenzen
1.24	spicy	['spaɪsi]	würzig, pikant
	noodle	['nuːdl]	Nudel
	gallery	['gæləri]	Galerie
3	compliment	['kɒmplɪmənt]	Kompliment
	lifestyle	['laɪfstaɪl]	Lebensstil
4	blank	[blæŋk]	leer, unbeschrieben
	preference	['prefrəns]	Vorliebe
	to fish	[fɪʃ]	fischen, angeln
	vegetarian	[ˌvedʒə'teəriən]	vegetarisch
	to pick	[pɪk]	aussuchen, auswählen
	collage	['kɒlɑːʒ]	Collage

| to **discover** | [dɪˈskʌvə] | entdecken |
| to **refuse** | [ˈrefjuːs] | ablehnen |

UNIT 3, Extra practice

2	**experienced**	[ɪkˈspɪəriənst]	erfahren
3	**lobby**	[ˈlɒbi]	Eingangshalle, Foyer
4	**logical**	[ˈlɒdʒɪkl]	logisch
	sequence	[ˈsiːkwəns]	Reihenfolge
5	**tie**	[taɪ]	Krawatte
	male	[meɪl]	männlich
6	**landing**	[ˈlændɪŋ]	Landung
	fog	[fɒg]	Nebel
CS	to **get down to business**	[get daʊn tə ˈbɪznəs]	zum Geschäftlichen übergehen
	ordinary	[ˈɔːdnri]	gewöhnlich, alltäglich
	to **talk shop**	[tɔːk ˈʃɒp]	über die Arbeit reden / fachsimpeln
	to **come across**	[ˌkʌm əˈkrɒs]	(auf andere) wirken
	abrupt	[əˈbrʌpt]	schroff, brüsk
	uncomfortable	[ʌnˈkʌmftəbl]	unangenehm, peinlich
	genuine	[ˈdʒenjuɪn]	aufrichtig, echt
	beforehand	[bɪˈfɔːhænd]	vorher, im Voraus
	superficial	[ˌsuːpəˈfɪʃl]	oberflächlich
	worthwhile	[ˌwɜːθˈwaɪl]	lohnend

Small talk

Is this your first visit to …?	Ist dies Ihr erster Besuch in …?
Is there anything in particular that …?	Gibt es etwas Besonderes, das …?
What's life like in …?	Wie ist das Leben in …?
How about …?	Wie wäre es (mit) …?
I'd love to.	Das würde ich sehr gerne machen.
That would be nice/lovely.	Das wäre schön.
Well, only if we have enough time.	Nun, nur falls wir genug Zeit haben.
Actually, I'd prefer not to …	Eigentlich würde ich lieber nicht …
to get down to business / to talk shop	zum Geschäftlichen übergehen / über Geschäftliches reden
Is it true that …?	Stimmt es, dass …?
Could you tell me more about …?	Könnten Sie mir mehr über … erzählen?
So, what do you think about …?	Also, was denken Sie über …?

UNIT 4, Part A

	to **look** ahead	[ˌlʊk əˈhed]	in die Zukunft blicken
▶	**famous** for	[ˈfeɪməs fə]	berühmt für
1	**factfile**	[ˈfæktfaɪl]	Steckbrief
	premier	[ˈpremɪə]	Spitzen-, Top-, führend
	net	[net]	netto, Netto-
	turnover	[ˈtɜːnəʊvə]	Umsatz
	bn = **billion**	[ˈbɪljən]	Milliarde
1.26	**segment**	[ˈsegmənt]	Segment, Teil
	farmer	[ˈfɑːmə]	Landwirt/in
	affected	[əˈfektɪd]	betroffen
	past	[pɑːst]	letzte/r/s *(zeitlich)*
	due to sth	[ˈdjuː tə]	aufgrund von etw
	pressure	[ˈpreʃə]	Druck
	market pressure	[ˈmɑːkɪt preʃə]	Marktdruck
	lost	[lɒst]	verloren
	to **force**	[fɔːs]	zwingen
	to **cause**	[kɔːz]	verursachen
	to **bring out**	[brɪŋ ˈaʊt]	herausbringen
	high-end	[ˌhaɪˈend]	exklusiv
	unlike	[ˌʌnˈlaɪk]	anders als
	average	[ˈævərɪdʒ]	Durchschnitts-, durchschnittlich
	fair	[feə]	gerecht
	image	[ˈɪmɪdʒ]	Image, Bild
	to **push up**	[ˌpʊʃ ˈʌp]	in die Höhe treiben
	most likely	[məʊst ˈlaɪkli]	wahrscheinlich
	to **balance**	[ˈbæləns]	ausgleichen, aufwiegen
	overall	[ˌəʊvərˈɔːl]	allgemein, gesamt, Gesamt-
	loss	[lɒs]	Verlust
	to **be** in **for** sth	[bi ˈɪn fə]	etw zu erwarten haben
	whatever	[wɒtˈevə]	was auch immer
2	**intention**	[ɪnˈtenʃn]	Absicht, Vorsatz
	to **predict**	[prɪˈdɪkt]	vorher-/voraussagen, prophezeien
	be **based** on sth	[ˈbeɪst ɒn]	auf etw basieren
	sign	[saɪn]	Zeichen
	to **eat out**	[ˌiːt ˈaʊt]	essen gehen
5	to **chair**	[tʃeə]	den Vorsitz haben, leiten
6	**as follows**	[əz ˈfɒləʊz]	wie folgt
	overview	[ˈəʊvəvjuː]	Überblick
	to **face** sth	[feɪs]	mit etw konfrontiert werden
	to **bring** sb **up to speed**	[brɪŋ ˌʌp tə ˈspiːd]	jmdn auf den neuesten Stand bringen

	forecast	['fɔːkɑːst]	Prognose, Voraussage
	to define	[dɪ'faɪn]	definieren
	to be set in stone	[ˌset ɪn 'stəʊn]	unverrückbar sein
	to finalize	['faɪnəlaɪz]	festlegen, beschließen
	issue	['ɪʃuː]	Frage, Thema
7	approximately	[ə'prɒksɪmətli]	nahezu, fast
1.27	to peak	[piːk]	den Höhepunkt/die Spitze erreichen
	concept	['kɒnsept]	Konzept
	unfortunately	[ʌn'fɔːtʃənətli]	unglücklicherweise
	unexpectedly	[ˌʌnɪk'spektɪdli]	unerwartet
	in time	[ɪn 'taɪm]	rechtzeitig
	to interrupt	[ˌɪntə'rʌpt]	unterbrechen
	union	['juːniən]	Vereinigung, Verband
	to break	[breɪk]	brechen, verletzen
	cooperative	[kəʊ'ɒpərətɪv]	Genossenschaft
9	line graph	['laɪn ɡræf]	Liniendiagramm
	to level off	[ˌlevl 'ɒf]	sich einpendeln, gleich bleiben

Talking about sales figures

Sales rose steadily.	Die Verkaufszahlen stiegen stetig.
First quarter sales were around …	Im ersten Quartal lagen die Verkaufszahlen bei ungefähr …
Second quarter sales continued to rise.	Im zweiten Quartal stiegen die Verkaufszahlen weiter an.
Sales peaked at …	Die Verkaufszahlen erreichten bei … ihren Höhepunkt.
Sales fell sharply/slightly.	Die Verkaufszahlen fielen steil/leicht ab.

UNIT 4, Part B

	installation	[ˌɪnstə'leɪʃn]	Installation, Einrichtung, Einbau
1			
1.28	testing	['testɪŋ]	Testen, Prüfen
	ongoing	['ɒngəʊɪŋ]	fortlaufend, andauernd
	trial	['traɪəl]	Test, Probe
	phase	[feɪz]	Phase
	optimization	[ˌɒptɪmaɪ'zeɪʃn]	Optimierung
	fitted	['fɪtɪd]	*hier:* eingerichtet, angepasst
	operator	['ɒpəreɪtə]	Bediener/in, Anwender/in
2	in-house	[ˌɪn 'haʊs]	intern, innerbetrieblich
	memo	['meməʊ]	Kurzmitteilung, Aktennotiz
5	projection	[prə'dʒekʃn]	Voraussage, Prognose
1.29	unrealistic	[ˌʌnriːə'lɪstɪk]	unrealistisch
	changeover	[ˌtʃeɪndʒəʊvə]	Übergang, Umstellung

	to arise	[ə'raɪz]	entstehen, sich ergeben
	shift	[ʃɪft]	Schicht
	to calm down	[ˌkɑːm 'daʊn]	sich beruhigen
	back-up	['bækʌp]	Reserve, Ersatz
	to stay on schedule	[ˌsteɪ ɒn 'ʃedjuːl]	im Zeitplan bleiben
	transition	[træn'zɪʃn]	Übergang
	standby	['stændbaɪ]	Reserve
	on standby	[ɒn 'stændbaɪ]	in Bereitschaft
	in case	[ɪn 'keɪs]	für den Fall
	whole	[həʊl]	ganz
	figure	['fɪgə]	Zahl
	to go over sth	[ˌgəʊ 'əʊvə]	etw durchgehen, durchsehen
	concern	[kən'sɜːn]	Bedenken, Besorgnis
7	to select	[sɪ'lekt]	auswählen
	to block	[blɒk]	blockieren, sperren
	morale	[mə'rɑːl]	*hier:* Stimmung

Discussing in a meeting

I agree with you up to a point.	Bis zu einem gewissen Punkt stimme ich mit Ihnen überein.
I'm afraid I have to disagree.	Leider kann ich nicht zustimmen.
Sorry to interrupt.	Entschuldigen Sie, dass ich Sie unterbreche.
What exactly do you mean by …?	Was genau meinen Sie mit …?
Are you saying that …	Wollen Sie sagen, dass …
I understand your concern.	Ich verstehe Ihre Bedenken.
I'll get back to you.	Ich sage Ihnen Bescheid.

UNIT 4, Business file

1	to get sth right	[ˌget 'raɪt]	etw richtig verstehen
	giveaway	['gɪvəweɪ]	Werbeartikel
	logo	['ləʊgəʊ]	Logo
	light	[laɪt]	hell
	white	[waɪt]	weiß
	memory stick	['meməri stɪk]	USB-Stick
	mug	[mʌg]	Tasse
	X-ray	['eksreɪ]	Röntgenstrahl
	Yankee	['jæŋki]	Nordstaatler
2	to press	[pres]	drücken
1.31	query	['kwɪəri]	Frage
	menu	['menjuː]	Menü
	notepaper	['nəʊtpeɪpə]	Briefpapier

term	[tɜːm]	Bedingung
terms of payment	[ˌtɜːmz əv ˈpeɪmənt]	Zahlungsbedingungen
satisfied	[ˈsætɪsfaɪd]	zufrieden
handling	[ˈhændlɪŋ]	Abwicklung, Bearbeitung
handling costs	[ˈhændlɪŋ kɒsts]	Abwicklungskosten, Bearbeitungskosten
exception	[ɪkˈsepʃn]	Ausnahme
anything else	[ˌeniθɪŋ ˈels]	noch etwas
on file	[ɒn ˈfaɪl]	in den Akten
lead time	[ˈliːd taɪm]	Bearbeitungszeit, Lieferzeit

3 due　　　　　　　　[djuː]　　　　　　　fällig

UNIT 4, Extra practice

2 spare　　　　　[speə]　　　　　　Ersatz-
　bird　　　　　　[bɜːd]　　　　　　Vogel
3 though　　　　　[ðəʊ]　　　　　trotzdem, aber, dennoch
　postcard　　　　[ˈpəʊstkɑːd]　　Postkarte
cs polite　　　　　[pəˈlaɪt]　　　　höflich
　politeness　　　[pəˈlaɪtnəs]　　Höflichkeit
　indirectness　　[ˌɪndəˈrektnəs]　Indirektheit
　to complain　　[kəmˈpleɪn]　　sich beschweren
　to state　　　　[steɪt]　　　　erklären, darstellen
　rather　　　　　[ˈrɑːðə]　　　　eher, lieber
　to blame　　　　[bleɪm]　　　　beschuldigen
　apparently　　　[əˈpærəntli]　　anscheinend, scheinbar
　to soften　　　　[ˈsɒfn]　　　　abschwächen
　bossy　　　　　[ˈbɒsi]　　　　rechthaberisch
　to avoid　　　　[əˈvɔɪd]　　　　vermeiden
　kindly　　　　　[ˈkaɪndli]　　　freundlicherweise

UNIT 5, Part A

comparison	[kəmˈpærɪsn]	Vergleich
tag	[tæg]	Schild, Etikett
to bargain	[ˈbɑːgɪn]	verhandeln, handeln
bulk	[bʌlk]	Menge, Masse
to motivate	[ˈməʊtɪveɪt]	motivieren
healthy	[ˈhelθi]	gesund
commitment	[kəˈmɪtmənt]	Einsatz, Engagement
well-being	[ˈwelbiːɪŋ]	Wohlbefinden
half-trying	[ˌhɑːf ˈtraɪɪŋ]	halbherzig
used	[juːzd]	gebraucht

insurance	[ɪnˈʃʊərəns]	Versicherung
in total	[ɪn ˈtəʊtl]	insgesamt
to use sth up	[juːz ˈʌp]	etw aufbrauchen
entire	[ɪnˈtaɪə]	ganze/r/s
weights	[weɪts]	Gewichte
weights machine	[ˈweɪts məʃiːn]	Trainingsgerät mit Gewichten
additional	[əˈdɪʃənl]	zusätzlich
top floor	[ˈtɒp flɔː]	oberste Etage

2	incorrect	[ˌɪnkəˈrekt]	nicht korrekt
	membership	[ˈmembəʃɪp]	Mitgliedschaft
3	less likely	[les ˈlaɪkli]	unwahrscheinlich
	to injure	[ˈɪndʒə]	sich verletzen
	trained	[treɪnd]	trainiert, geschult
	to travel	[ˈtrævl]	*hier:* hinfahren
	to care about sth	[ˈkeə əbaʊt]	sich um etw sorgen, kümmern
5	confused	[kənˈfjuːzd]	verwirrt
ⓘ 1.34	feasible	[ˈfiːzəbl]	machbar, möglich
	to drive a hard bargain	[draɪv ə ˌhɑːd ˈbɑːgən]	hart verhandeln
	however	[haʊˈevə]	wie auch immer
	to throw in	[ˌθrəʊ ˈɪn]	(gratis) dazugeben
	mat	[mæt]	Matte
	to re-issue	[ˌriːˈɪʃuː]	neu ausstellen, neu auflegen
	meanwhile	[ˈmiːnwaɪl]	inzwischen
	tough	[tʌf]	zäh, ausdauernd, hart
	negotiator	[nɪˈgəʊʃieɪtə]	Händler/in
	approval	[əˈpruːvl]	Zustimmung
	proposal	[prəˈpəʊzl]	Vorschlag

Negociating a deal

We might be able to … if you …	Wir könnten … wenn Sie …
How does that sound?	Wie hört sich das an?
That sounds fair/acceptable.	Das hört sich fair/akzeptabel an.
I might be able to agree to that.	Dem könnte ich zustimmen.
Now it's getting interesting.	Jetzt wird es interessant.
You drive a hard bargain.	Sie verhandeln hart.
I'm sorry, that's not feasible.	Es tut mir leid, das ist nicht machbar.
I can't increase the discount /	Ich kann keinen höheren Nachlass geben /
I can't lower the price.	ich kann den Preis nicht weiter senken.
I can throw in …	Ich kann … dazugeben/drauflegen.

6	to reject	[rɪ'dʒekt]	ablehnen, zurückweisen
7	flexibility	[ˌfleksə'bɪləti]	Flexibilität
	walk-away point	[ˌwɔːk ə'weɪ pɔɪnt]	Schmerzgrenze
	vice versa	[ˌvaɪs 'vɜːsə]	umgekehrt
	party	['pɑːti]	Partei
	impossible	[ɪm'pɒsəbl]	unmöglich
	winner	['wɪnə]	Gewinner/in
	room	[ruːm]	*hier:* Platz
	preparation	[ˌprepə'reɪʃn]	Vorbereitung
	to benefit	['benɪfɪt]	profitieren
	acceptable	[ək'septəbl]	akzeptabel
	greatly	['greɪtli]	sehr, stark
	to influence	['ɪnfluəns]	beeinflussen
	as they say	[əz ˌðeɪ 'seɪ]	wie man sagt
	to fail	[feɪl]	scheitern, missglücken
9	asking price	['ɑːskɪŋ praɪs]	geforderter Preis
	specially	['speʃəli]	speziell
	layout	['leɪaʊt]	Anordnung, Aufteilung
	to advertise	['ædvətaɪz]	ankündigen, zum Verkauf anbieten

UNIT 5, Part B

▶	to maintain	[meɪn'teɪn]	bewahren, aufrecht erhalten
1	workload	['wɜːkləʊd]	Arbeitspensum
🔊 1.38	to be into sth	[bi 'ɪntə]	sich für etw interessieren
	lazy	['leɪzi]	faul
	to burn out	[bɜːn 'aʊt]	ausbrennen, sich kaputt machen
	counterproductive	[ˌkaʊntəprə'dʌktɪv]	kontraproduktiv
	satisfaction	[ˌsætɪs'fækʃn]	Zufriedenheit, Befriedigung
2	enjoyable	[ɪn'dʒɔɪəbl]	angenehm, unterhaltsam
🔊 1.39	to give sth a go	[gɪv ə 'gəʊ]	etw ausprobieren
	front door	[ˌfrʌnt 'dɔː]	Vordertür

Persuading

How about …?	Wie wäre es, wenn …?
Why don't you try …?	Warum probieren Sie nicht mal …?
Come on!	Kommen Sie schon! Auf geht's!
I'll give it a go.	Ich probier's mal.

3	useless	['juːsləs]	nutzlos
5	to text	[tekst]	eine SMS schreiben

	to **have second thoughts**	[həv ˌsekənd 'θɔːts]	es sich anders überlegen, Zweifel haben
	to **shorten**	['ʃɔːtn]	verkürzen, kürzen
	to **remove**	[rɪ'muːv]	wegnehmen, entfernen
	fix	[fɪks]	fest
6	to **own**	[əʊn]	besitzen
	abbreviation	[əˌbriːvi'eɪʃn]	Abkürzung
	follower	['fɒləʊə]	Anhänger/in
	effective	[ɪ'fektɪv]	wirksam, effektiv
	to **hurt**	[hɜːt]	verletzen, schaden
7	**economy**	[ɪ'kɒnəmi]	Wirtschaft
	stressed	[strest]	gestresst
	to **ignore**	[ɪg'nɔː]	ignorieren
	out of balance	[aʊt əv 'bæləns]	aus dem Gleichgewicht
	walking lunch	[wɔːkɪŋ 'lʌntʃ]	Spaziergang in der Mittagspause
	to **concentrate**	['kɒnsntreɪt]	sich konzentrieren
8	**parental**	[pə'rentl]	elterlich
	parental leave	[pə'rentl liːv]	Elternzeit, Erziehungsurlaub
	phased	[feɪzd]	gestuft
	retirement	[rɪ'taɪəmənt]	Ruhestand
	scheme	[skiːm]	Schema
	phased retirement	[ˌfeɪzd rɪ'taɪəmənt]	Altersteilzeit
	foundation	[faʊn'deɪʃn]	Stiftung
	improvement	[ɪm'pruːvmənt]	Verbesserung
	option	['ɒpʃn]	Möglichkeit, Option, Wahl
	on average	[ɒn 'ævərɪdʒ]	im Durchschnitt

UNIT 5, Business file

1	**selection**	[sɪ'lekʃn]	Auswahl
⏺ 1.40	**choice**	[tʃɔɪs]	Wahl, Entscheidung
	functionality	[ˌfʌŋkʃə'næləti]	Funktionalität
	ex-works	[eks 'wɜːks]	ab Werk
	breakdown	['breɪkdaʊn]	Aufschlüsselung
	fee	[fiː]	Gebühr
	COD = cash on delivery	[ˌsiː əʊ 'diː, kæʃ ɒn dɪ'lɪvəri]	Barzahlung bei Lieferung
	in full	[ɪn 'fʊl]	vollständig
	to **change your mind**	[ˌtʃeɪndʒ jɔː 'maɪnd]	es sich anders überlegen
	single	['sɪŋgl]	einfach
	fault	[fɔːlt]	Fehler, Schuld
	to **refund**	[rɪ'fʌnd]	rückerstatten, zurückzahlen
	rebate	['riːbeɪt]	Rabatt, Preisnachlass

in writing	[ɪn 'raɪtɪŋ]	schriftlich
cheque	[tʃek]	Scheck
against	[ə'genst]	gegen

3	enthusiast	[ɪn'θjuːziæst]	*hier:* Fan, Anhänger/in
	relatively	['relətɪvli]	relativ
	racquet	['rækɪt]	Schläger
	home movie theatre	[həʊm muːvi 'θɪətə]	Heimkino
	widescreen TV	[ˌwaɪdskriːn tiː 'viː]	Großbildfernseher

Talking about prices and terms

What do your prices include?	Was beinhalten Ihre Preise?
Are these the ex-works prices?	Sind dies die Preise ab Werk?
Do these prices include delivery/taxes?	Sind diese Preise inklusive Lieferung/Steuern?
What are your terms of payment?	Wie sind Ihre Zahlungsbedingungen?
What method(s) of payment do you accept?	Welche Zahlungsart(en) akzeptieren Sie?
Can you let me have this in writing?	Können Sie mir das schriftlich geben?
Payment is COD.	Barzahlung bei Lieferung.
We can give you a rebate.	Wir können Ihnen einen Rabatt einräumen.
We'll refund the money.	Wir erstatten das Geld.

UNIT 5, Extra practice

2	to **beat**	[biːt]	schlagen
	to **beat** sb to the market	[ˌbiːt tə ðə 'maːkɪt]	jmdn auf dem Markt/im Wettbewerb schlagen
3	to **celebrate**	['selɪbreɪt]	feiern
	champagne	[ʃæm'peɪn]	Champagner, Sekt
7	to **collocate**	['kɒləkeɪt]	kollokieren, zusammenstellen
9	**exaggerated**	[ɪg'zædzəreɪtɪd]	übertrieben
CS	to **stand for**	['stænd fə]	stehen für, bedeuten
	acronym	['ækrənɪm]	Abkürzung, Kurzwort

General abbreviations

am (ante meridiem)	vormittags
pm (post meridiem)	nachmittags
i.e. (it est)	das heißt
e.g. (exempli gratia)	zum Beispiel
approx. (approximately)	ungefähr
FAQ (frequently asked questions)	häufig gestellte Fragen
ATB (all the best)	alles Gute
pp (per procurationem)	im Auftrag

Business abbreviations

re (regarding)	betrifft, betreffend
asap (as soon as possible)	so bald wie möglich
VAT (value added tax)	Mehrwertsteuer
RSVP (Répondez à l'invitation s'il vous plaît.)	um Antwort wird gebeten
BTW (by the way)	übrigens
FYI (for your information)	zu Ihrer Information
IMO (in my opinion)	meines Erachtens

UNIT 6, Part A

1	to cross	[krɒs]	kreuzen
	to cross out	[ˌkrɒs 'aʊt]	streichen
	pioneering	[ˌpaɪə'nɪərɪŋ]	bahnbrechend
	leading	['liːdɪŋ]	führend
	challenging	['tʃælɪndʒɪŋ]	herausfordernd
	rewarding	[rɪ'wɔːdɪŋ]	lohnend
	adaptable	[ə'dæptəbl]	anpassungsfähig, flexibel
2	edge	[edʒ]	hier: Vorteil, Vorsprung
2.2	to highlight	['haɪlaɪt]	hervorheben, herausstellen
	diamond	['daɪəmənd]	Diamant
	drill	[drɪl]	Bohrer
	knife	[naɪf]	Messer
	blade	[bleɪd]	Klinge
	processing	['prəʊsesɪŋ]	Herstellung, Bearbeitung
	back in 2000	['bæk ɪn]	damals, im Jahr 2000
	whose	[huːz]	deren/dessen
	You name it!	[juː 'neɪm ɪt]	Alles, was du dir denken kannst.
	fluently	['fluːəntli]	fließend
	unfamiliar	[ˌʌnfə'mɪliə]	unbekannt
3	spouse	[spaʊz]	Ehepartner/in
4	track	[træk]	Pfad, Spur, Kurs
	track record	['træk rekɔːd]	Erfolgsgeschichte, Leistung
	addition	[ə'dɪʃn]	Bereicherung, Ergänzung
	thus	[ðʌs]	so, demzufolge
	afterwards	['ɑːftəwədz]	danach
	post	[pəʊst]	Posten
	eager	['iːgə]	begierig, lernfreudig
	to feature sb	['fiːtʃə]	hier: jmdn vorstellen
6	intriguing	[ɪn'triːgɪŋ]	faszinierend, verblüffend
	three-page	['θriː peɪdʒ]	dreiseitig
	editor	['edɪtə]	Herausgeber/in

to post	[pəʊst]	(online) posten
webinar	[webɪ'nɑ:]	interaktives Onlineseminar
stand-up	[ˌstænd 'ʌp]	Steh-
audiobook	['ɔːdiəʊbʊk]	Hörbuch

UNIT 6, Part B

	base	[beɪs]	(Baseball:) Mal, Base
	to touch base	[ˌtʌtʃ 'beɪs]	sich bei jmdm melden
	pitch	[pɪtʃ]	Wurf, hier: Präsentation, Verkaufsgespräch
1	demo	['deməʊ]	Vorführung
2.3	to convince	[kən'vɪns]	überzeugen
	to keep one's fingers crossed	[kiːp wʌnz ˌfɪŋgəz 'krɒst]	die Daumen drücken
	shame	[ʃeɪm]	Schande, Scham
	prototype	['prəʊtətaɪp]	Prototyp
	appraisal	[ə'preɪzl]	Beurteilung, Mitarbeitergespräch
2	briefly	['briːfli]	kurz
	someplace	['sʌmpleɪs]	irgendwohin
	progress	['prəʊgrəs]	Fortschritt
	in sight	[ɪn 'saɪt]	in Sicht
5	to notice	['nəʊtɪs]	bemerken
2.4	to reschedule	[ˌriː'ʃedjuːl]	verlegen
	it can't be helped	[ɪt ˌkɑːnt biː 'helpt]	es lässt sich nicht ändern
	to get in touch	[ˌget ɪn 'tʌtʃ]	kontaktieren
	to pick up	[ˌpɪk 'ʌp]	abholen
6	to confuse	[kən'fjuːz]	durcheinanderbringen
	to chew	[tʃuː]	kauen
	to chop	[tʃɒp]	hacken, klein schneiden

Reporting progress

We've done …, but we haven't … yet.	Wir haben … erledigt, aber wir haben noch nicht …
There's still quite a bit/not much left to do.	Es gibt noch ziemlich viel/nicht mehr viel zu tun.
We've made excellent progress.	Wir haben großartige Fortschritte gemacht.
We've done practically everything.	Wir haben eigentlich alles erledigt.
We're almost there.	Wir haben es fast geschafft.
The end is in sight.	Das Ende ist in Sicht.

UNIT 6, Business file

1	I can't make it.	[aɪ ˌkɑːnt ˈmeɪk ɪt]	Ich schaffe es nicht.
2.7	particularly	[pəˈtɪkjələli]	besonders
2.8	to come up	[ˌkʌm ˈʌp]	dazwischenkommen
	Never mind.	[ˌnevə ˈmaɪnd]	Macht nichts.
	to suppose	[səˈpəʊz]	annehmen, glauben
	although	[ɔːlˈðəʊ]	obwohl
	to pencil sth in	[ˌpensl ˈɪn]	vormerken
	to assume	[əˈsjuːm]	annehmen, vermuten
2.9	glorious	[ˈɡlɔːriəs]	fantastisch
	to surf	[sɜːf]	surfen
	as a matter of fact	[əz ə ˌmætər əv ˈfækt]	in der Tat, tatsächlich
	to hold on	[ˌhəʊld ˈɒn]	warten
2.10	to fit sb in	[ˌfɪt ˈɪn]	*hier:* jmdn unterbringen
	indicated	[ˈɪndɪkeɪtɪd]	angezeigt, markiert
	to suit	[suːt]	passen
	provisional	[prəˈvɪʒənl]	provisorisch, vorläufig
	unexpected	[ˌʌnɪkˈspektɪd]	unerwartet
2	inbox	[ˈɪnbɒks]	Postfach-Eingang
	double-booked	[ˌdʌbl ˈbʊkt]	*hier:* mehrfach verabredet
	to propose	[prəˈpəʊz]	vorschlagen
3	alternative	[ɔːlˈtɜːnətɪv]	alternativ

Making an appointment

What time would suit you?	Wann würde es Ihnen passen?
Are you free on …?	Haben Sie am … Zeit?
Can you make it tomorrow?	Schaffen Sie es morgen?
When is it convenient for you?	Wann ist es Ihnen recht?
Sorry, but … is inconvenient for me.	Entschuldigung, aber … passt mir nicht.
Shall we make a provisional appointment?	Sollen wir einen vorläufigen Termin machen?
Shall we pencil that in?	Sollen wir das vormerken?

Changing an appointment

Can't we just cancel this appointment and …?	Können wir diesen Termin nicht absagen und …?
Unfortunately, something unexpected has come up.	Leider ist etwas Unvorhergesehenes dazwischengekommen.
Can we find an alternative time?	Können wir einen anderen Termin/ Zeitpunkt finden?

UNIT 6, Extra practice

2	onto	[ˈɒntə]	auf
3	exotic	[ɪɡˈzɒtɪk]	exotisch
7	shin	[ʃɪn]	Schienbein
◐ 2.11	chin	[tʃɪn]	Kinn
8	extensive	[ɪkˈstensɪv]	umfassend
	properly	[ˈprɒpəli]	richtig, anständig
cs	to matter	[ˈmætə]	wichtig sein, einen Unterschied machen
	pause	[pɔːz]	Pause
	explanation	[ˌekspləˈneɪʃn]	Erklärung
	humour	[ˈhjuːmə]	Humor, Komik
	shrug	[ʃrʌg]	mit den Achseln zucken
	amusing	[əˈmjuːzɪŋ]	lustig
	account	[əˈkaʊnt]	Bericht
	to delay	[dɪˈleɪ]	aufhalten, verzögern
	one-liner	[ˈwʌnlaɪnə]	Einzeiler
	to believe	[bɪˈliːv]	glauben
	traffic	[ˈtræfɪk]	Verkehr
	to overdo	[ˌəʊvəˈduː]	übertreiben

UNIT 7, Part A

	to present	[prɪˈzent]	präsentieren
1	to pay back	[ˌpeɪ ˈbæk]	zurückzahlen
	certain	[ˈsɜːtn]	gewiss, bestimmt
	to borrow	[ˈbɒrəʊ]	sich leihen, sich borgen
	property	[ˈprɒpəti]	Eigentum, Immobilie
	interest rate	[ˈɪntrəst reɪt]	Zinsen
	mortgage	[ˈmɔːɡɪdʒ]	Hypothek
	loan	[ləʊn]	Darlehen
◐ 2.12	holding	[ˈhəʊldɪŋ]	Anteil
	holding company	[ˈhəʊldɪŋ kʌmpəni]	Holdinggesellschaft
	to acquire	[əˈkwaɪə]	erwerben
	touch	[tʌtʃ]	Note, Touch
2	disappointing	[ˌdɪsəˈpɔɪntɪŋ]	enttäuschend
3	anymore	[eniˈmɔː]	nicht mehr
4	series	[ˈsɪəriːz]	Serie, Reihe
6	so far	[ˌsəʊ ˈfɑː]	bis jetzt, bisher
	capital	[ˈkæpɪtl]	Kapital
	entry	[ˈentri]	Eintritt

7	track	[træk]	Kurs
2.13	to look around	[ˌlʊk əˈraʊnd]	herumschauen
	to stop by	[ˌstɒp ˈbaɪ]	vorbeikommen
	indoors	[ˈɪndɔːz]	drinnen
8	mutual	[ˈmjuːtʃʊəl]	beiderseitig, gemeinsam
	acquaintance	[əˈkweɪntəns]	der/die Bekannte
	to act out	[ˌækt ˈaʊt]	durchspielen
	Take care!	[ˌteɪk ˈkeə]	Mach's gut! Pass auf dich auf!

Saying goodbye

Thanks for coming.	Danke, dass Sie gekommen sind.
It's been good seeing you.	Es war schön, Sie zu sehen.
Please say hello / give my regards to …	Grüßen Sie bitte … von mir.
Would you like me to call you a taxi?	Soll ich Ihnen ein Taxi rufen?
Enjoy the rest of your time here.	Genießen Sie Ihren restlichen Aufenthalt hier.
Have a good trip home.	Gute Heimreise.
Take care. Let's keep in touch (about …).	Machen Sie es gut. Lassen Sie uns (wegen …) in Kontakt bleiben.

UNIT 7, Part B

▶	advantage	[ədˈvɑːntɪdʒ]	Vorteil
	disadvantage	[ˌdɪsədˈvɑːntɪdʒ]	Nachteil
1	to send up	[ˌsend ˈʌp]	hochschicken
2.14	to wake up	[ˌweɪk ˈʌp]	aufwachen
	wake up call	[ˈweɪk ʌp kɒl]	Weckruf
2.15	peanuts	[ˈpiːnʌts]	Erdnüsse
2.16	to clear	[klɪə]	hier: abräumen
	meat	[miːt]	Fleisch
	leaf	[liːf]	Blatt
	asparagus	[əˈspærəgəs]	Spargel
	barman	[ˈbɑːmən]	Barkeeper
	trouble	[ˈtrʌbl]	Schwierigkeiten, Ärger, Probleme
2	to have left	[həv ˈleft]	übrig haben
3	non-smoking	[ˌnɒn ˈsməʊkɪŋ]	Nichtraucher-
	dish	[dɪʃ]	Gericht
4	table	[ˈteɪbl]	hier: Tabelle
2.17	Chianti	[kiˈænti]	Chianti
	still water	[ˌstɪl ˈwɔːtə]	Wasser ohne Kohlensäure
	sparkling water	[ˌspɑːklɪŋ ˈwɔːtə]	kohlensäurehaltiges Mineralwasser
2.18	set	[set]	Set, Satz, Paar, Garnitur
	cutlery	[ˈkʌtləri]	Besteck

	Here you go.	[ˌhɪə jə ˈɡəʊ]	Bitte schön.
	draught	[drɑːft]	Luftzug
	back	[bæk]	Hinterseite, Rückseite
	to blow	[bləʊ]	blasen, wehen
2.19	to overcook	[ˌəʊvəˈkʊk]	verkochen
	to sort out	[ˌsɔːt ˈaʊt]	in Ordnung bringen, aufräumen
	medium rare	[ˌmiːdiəm ˈreə]	*Steak:* halb durchgebraten
	handbag	[ˈhændbæg]	Handtasche

Polite requests and complaints

Excuse me, could you please …?	Entschuldigen Sie, könnten Sie bitte …?
I was wondering if we could …	Ich habe mich gefragt, ob wir … könnten.
Would it be possible to …?	Wäre es möglich …?
I am sorry to say that …	Leider muss ich sagen …

5	thirsty	[ˈθɜːsti]	durstig
	salt sticks	[ˈsɔːlt stɪks]	Salzstangen
	to solve	[sɒlv]	lösen
	bill	[bɪl]	Rechnung
	printout	[ˈprɪntaʊt]	Ausdruck
	travel expenses	[ˈtrævl ɪkspensɪz]	Reisekosten
	salted	[ˈsɔːltɪd]	gesalzen
	to calculate	[ˈkælkjuleɪt]	berechnen, ausrechnen
	portion	[ˈpɔːʃn]	Portion
6	virtual	[ˈvɜːtʃuəl]	virtuell
	to conduct	[kɒnˈdʌkt]	führen
	offsite	[ˌɒfˈsaɪt]	extern
	physical	[ˈfɪzɪkl]	körperlich, physisch
	kick-off	[ˈkɪkɒf]	Start, Anfang
	so-called	[ˌsəʊ ˈkɔːld]	sogenannte/r/s
	to put out the fire	[pʊt ˌaʊt ðə ˈfaɪə]	die Wogen glätten
	to be back on track	[bi ˌbæk ɒn ˈtræk]	wieder auf dem richtigen Weg sein
	sensitive	[ˈsensətɪv]	heikel
	to set up	[ˌset ˈʌp]	arrangieren, einrichten
	to communicate	[kəˈmjuːnɪkeɪt]	kommunizieren
	via	[ˈvaɪə]	über, per, via
	to schedule	[ˈʃedjuːl]	ansetzen, planen
	attendee	[əˌtenˈdiː]	Teilnehmer/in, Anwesende/r
	to log on	[ˌlɒg ˈɒn]	sich anmelden, einwählen
	headset	[ˈhedset]	Kopfhörer
	to turn off	[ˌtɜːn ˈɒf]	ausschalten
	bandwidth	[ˈbændwɪdθ]	Bandbreite

to upload	[ˌʌpˈləʊd]	hochladen

UNIT 7, Business file

2	technique	[tekˈniːk]	Technik, Methode
	purpose	[ˈpɜːpəs]	Zweck, Absicht
	to reformulate	[ˌriːˈfɔːmjuleɪt]	umformulieren
	rhetorical	[rɪˈtɒrɪkl]	rhetorisch
	to refer to	[rɪˈfɜː tə]	sich beziehen auf
	to outline	[ˈaʊtlaɪn]	skizzieren, umreißen
	to anticipate	[ænˈtɪsɪpeɪt]	erwarten, rechnen mit, vorhersehen
	attention	[əˈtenʃn]	Aufmerksamkeit
	aim	[eɪm]	Ziel, Absicht
	spontaneous	[spɒnˈteɪniəs]	spontan

Presenting I

to outline the benefits for the audience	die Vorteile für die Zuhörer aufzeigen
to get the audience thinking about …	die Zuhörer dazu bringen, über … nachzudenken
to put more attention on …	mehr Aufmerksamkeit auf … lenken
to spontaneously react to …	spontan auf … reagieren
to stress a point	ein Argument / etwas hervorheben

3	expense	[ɪkˈspens]	(Geld-)Ausgabe
	to allow for sth	[əˈlaʊ fə]	etw zulassen
	remote	[rɪˈməʊt]	weit entfernt
	platform	[ˈplætfɔːm]	Plattform
	basic	[ˈbeɪsɪk]	grundlegend, wesentlich, Basis-
	volunteer	[ˌvɒlənˈtɪə]	Freiwillige/r
	body language	[ˈbɒdi læŋgwɪdʒ]	Körpersprache
	rapport	[ræˈpɔː]	Verhältnis
	furthermore	[ˌfɜːðəˈmɔː]	des Weiteren, außerdem
	simultaneous	[ˌsɪmlˈteɪniəs]	gleichzeitig, simultan

2.20

Presenting II

Introduction

I'd like to tell you about / explain …	Ich würde Ihnen gerne von … berichten / … erklären.
There are three main points I'd like to make.	Ich möchte hauptsächlich über drei Punkte sprechen.
My presentation will take around 20 minutes.	Meine Präsentation wird ungefähr 20 Minuten dauern.

Main part

That brings us to the next point …	Das bringt uns zum nächsten Punkt …
In other words …	Mit anderen Worten …
The slide gives you an overview of …	Die Folie gibt Ihnen einen Überblick über …
I'd like to draw your attention to …	Ich möchte Ihre Aufmerksamkeit auf … lenken.
… as you can see on the right/left.	… wie Sie links/rechts sehen können.

Ending

That brings me to the end (of my presentation).	Das bringt mich zum Ende (meiner Präsentation).
Feel free to ask any questions.	Fragen Sie ruhig.
Are there any questions?	Gibt es Fragen?
Thanks, that's a good question.	Danke, das ist eine gute Frage.
I thought you might ask that.	Ich dachte mir, dass Sie das vielleicht fragen würden.
It's as easy as that.	So einfach ist das.

4	couple	['kʌpl]	Paar
	renovation	[ˌrenə'veɪʃn]	Renovierung
	honeymoon	['hʌnimuːn]	Hochzeitsreise, Flitterwochen
	to draw sb's attention to sth	[ˌdrɔː ə'tenʃn tə]	jmds Aufmerksamkeit auf etw lenken
5	presenter	[prɪ'zentə]	Moderator/in, Referent/in

UNIT 7, Extra practice

1	the day before yesterday	[ðə ˌdeɪ bɪfɔː 'jestədeɪ]	vorgestern
5	today's special	[təˌdeɪz 'speʃl]	Tagesgericht
cs	awkward	['ɔːkwəd]	ungünstig
	individual	[ˌɪndɪ'vɪdʒuəl]	Individuum, Einzelne/r
	trait	[treɪt]	Merkmal

UNIT 8, Part A

	eco	['iːkəʊ]	Öko-, Umwelt-
1	forthcoming	[ˌfɔːθ'kʌmɪŋ]	bevorstehend
2	detergent	[dɪ'tɜːdʒənt]	Waschmittel, Spülmittel
	solar panel	[ˌsəʊlə 'pænl]	Sonnenkollektor
	hybrid	['haɪbrɪd]	hybrid, Misch-
	to recycle	[ˌriː'saɪkl]	wiederverwerten
	tissue	['tɪʃuː]	Papiertaschentuch
	cotton	['kɒtn]	Baumwolle
	sustainable	[sə'steɪnəbl]	nachhaltig, umweltgerecht
	biodegradable	[ˌbaɪəʊdɪ'greɪdəbl]	biologisch abbaubar
	skin	[skɪn]	Haut
	to package	['pækɪdʒ]	verpacken
	pre-packaged	[ˌpriː'pækɪdʒd]	abgepackt
	reusable	[ˌriː'juːzəbl]	wiederverwendbar
	container	[kən'teɪnə]	Behälter, Gefäß
	renewable	[rɪ'njuːəbl]	erneuerbar
	provider	[prə'vaɪdə]	Anbieter/in
	pollution	[pə'luːʃn]	Verschmutzung
	tree	[triː]	Baum
	homeowner	['həʊməʊnə]	Hausbesitzer
	to cut	[kʌt]	*hier:* kürzen, senken
	roomy	['ruːmi]	geräumig
	drawback	['drɔːbæk]	Nachteil, Haken
3	outlet	['aʊtlet]	Laden, Geschäftsstelle
◉2.21	at the end of the day	[ət ði ˌend əv ðə 'deɪ]	letztendlich
4	superior	[suː'pɪəriə]	ausgezeichnet, hervorragend
◉2.22	wholesaler	['həʊlseɪlə]	Großhändler/in
	reasonable	['riːznəbl]	vernünftig
	at first glance	[ət fɜːst 'glɑːns]	auf den ersten Blick
	laundry	['lɔːndri]	Wäsche
	around	[ə'raʊnd]	*hier:* vorhanden, da
	to promote sth	[prə'məʊt]	für etw Werbung machen

Linking the features and benefits of products

This product …	Dieses Produkt …
is top of the range / is very good quality.	ist ein Spitzenprodukt / hat eine sehr gute Qualität.
is value for money / cost-effective / quite reasonably priced.	ist preiswert / kostengünstig / ziemlich preiswert.
appeals to …	spricht … an.
is made of …	ist aus … gemacht.
is safe to use because …	ist sicher in der Anwendung, weil …
is easy to understand.	ist einfach zu verstehen.
is not only …, but is also …	ist nicht nur …, sondern auch …
is … than ever before.	ist … als jemals zuvor.
seems … at first glance.	sieht auf den ersten Blick … aus.
sets the standard for …	legt Maßstäbe für … fest.

5	to **appeal**	[ə'piːl]	gefallen, ansprechen
	price-conscious	['praɪs kɒnʃəs]	preisbewusst
	well-off	[ˌwel 'ɒf]	wohlhabend
	steel	['stiːl]	Stahl
	recyclable	[ˌriː'saɪkləbl]	wiederverwendbar
	technologically	[ˌteknə'lɒdʒɪkli]	technologisch
	advanced	[əd'vɑːnst]	hochentwickelt, fortgeschritten
	therefore	['ðeəfɔː]	deshalb
	toxic	['tɒksɪk]	giftig
	to **be priced**	[bi 'praɪst]	kosten
	stain	[steɪn]	Fleck
6	**appearance**	[ə'pɪərəns]	Erscheinungsbild
	not only … but also …	[nɒt əʊnli bət 'ɔːlsəʊ]	nicht nur …, sondern auch …
7	**besides**	[bɪ'saɪdz]	außerdem
	moreover	[mɔːr'əʊvə]	zudem, ferner
	for instance	[fər 'ɪnstəns]	zum Beispiel
	such as	['sʌtʃ əz]	wie beispielsweise
	despite	[dɪ'spaɪt]	trotz
	nevertheless	[ˌnevəðə'les]	trotzdem
	nonetheless	[ˌnʌnðə'les]	trotzdem, nichtsdestoweniger
	on the other hand	[ɒn ði 'ʌðə hænd]	andererseits
	consequently	['kɒnsɪkwəntli]	folglich, deshalb
	conclusion	[kən'kluːʒn]	Schlussfolgerung
	to **sum up**	[ˌsʌm 'ʌp]	resümieren, zusammenfassen
	organizer	['ɔːgənaɪzə]	Organisator/in, Veranstalter/in
	lighting equipment	['laɪtɪŋ ɪkwɪpmənt]	Lichtausrüstung
	to **manage sth**	['mænɪdʒ]	etw schaffen, gelingen

to attract	[əˈtrækt]	anziehen, auf sich ziehen
substantial	[səbˈstænʃl]	beträchtlich, erheblich
awareness	[əˈweənəs]	Bewusstsein
to rephrase	[ˌriːˈfreɪz]	umformulieren, anders ausdrücken

Linking words

also/and/besides	auch/und/außerdem
moreover / furthermore / in addition	darüber hinaus
for example / for instance / such as	zum Beispiel / wie zum Beispiel
although/but	obwohl / aber, sondern
however/still	wie auch immer / nach wie vor
despite the fact that / nevertheless / nonetheless	trotz der Tatsache, dass / nichtsdestotrotz / nichtsdestoweniger
on the one hand – on the other hand	einerseits – andererseits
as a result of / because of	in Folge (von) / wegen
so/thus	also/demzufolge
due to (this fact)	aufgrund (der Tatsache)
consequently / in conclusion	dadurch/folglich
to sum up / to summarize	schließlich / um zusammenzufassen

| 9 | framework | [ˈfreɪmwɜːk] | Rahmen |
| | consequence | [ˈkɒnsɪkwəns] | Konsequenz, Folge |

UNIT 8, Part B

▶	hard	[hɑːd]	schwer
1	comment	[ˈkɒment]	Kommentar
2.23	from ... onwards	[frəm ˈɒnwədz]	von ... an
2.24	stand-alone	[ˈstænd ələʊn]	alleinstehend, freistehend
	counter	[ˈkaʊntə]	Tresen, Schalter
	representative	[ˌreprɪˈzentətɪv]	Vertreter/in
	voicemail	[ˈvɔɪsmeɪl]	Mailbox
2	to replace	[rɪˈpleɪs]	ersetzen, austauschen
	at the latest	[ət ðə ˈleɪtəst]	spätestens
3	tablet	[ˈtæblət]	hier: Tablette
	concentrate	[ˈkɒnsntreɪt]	Konzentrat
	assortment	[əˈsɔːtmənt]	Auswahl
	drum	[drʌm]	Trommel, Fass
	colloquial	[kəˈləʊkwiəl]	umgangssprachlich
	slang	[slæŋ]	Slang, Jargon
	complex	[ˈkɒmpleks]	komplex, kompliziert
	neck of the woods (coll.)	[ˌnek əv ðə ˈwʊdz]	Gegend

4	to **invoice sb**	[ˈɪnvɔɪs]	jmdm eine Rechnung ausstellen
	to **query**	[ˈkwɪəri]	fragen
	to **succeed**	[səkˈsiːd]	Erfolg haben, erfolgreich sein
	to **enquire**	[ɪnˈkwaɪə]	untersuchen, sich erkundigen
	to **realize**	[ˈrɪəlaɪz]	bemerken, realisieren
	to **go out of business**	[gəʊ aʊt əv ˈbɪznəs]	Konkurs gehen
	to **pronounce**	[prəˈnaʊns]	aussprechen
	to **project**	[ˈprɒdʒekt]	planen

UNIT 8, Business file

1	**electric**	[ɪˈlektrɪk]	Elektro-, elektrisch
	classic	[ˈklæsɪk]	klassisch
	all-round	[ˌɔːlˈraʊnd]	vielseitig, Allround-
	model	[ˈmɒdl]	Modell
	step	[step]	*hier:* Einstieg
	feminine	[ˈfemənɪn]	weiblich, feminin
	playful	[ˈpleɪfl]	verspielt
	shocking	[ˈʃɒkɪŋ]	schockierend
	shocking pink	[ˌʃɒkɪŋ ˈpɪŋk]	grelles Pink
	speed	[spiːd]	*hier:* Gang
	adventurous	[ədˈventʃərəs]	abenteuerlustig
3	**foldable**	[ˈfəʊldəbl]	klappbar
	to **undertake**	[ˌʌndəˈteɪk]	vornehmen, durchführen
	to **take into account**	[teɪk ɪntu əˈkaʊnt]	berücksichtigen
	to **discontinue**	[ˌdɪskənˈtɪnjuː]	abbrechen, einstellen
5	to **examine**	[ɪgˈzæmɪn]	untersuchen
	to **contrast**	[kɒnˈtrɑːst]	vergleichen, gegenüberstellen
	finding	[ˈfaɪndɪŋ]	Ergebnis, Befund
	to **encounter sth**	[ɪnˈkaʊntə]	auf etw stoßen
	speculation	[ˌspekjuˈleɪʃn]	Spekulation, Vermutung
	taste	[teɪst]	Geschmack
	in the light of	[ɪn ðə ˈlaɪt əv]	angesichts

Writing a report

My boss requested this report on ...	Mein Chef hat diesen Bericht über ... angefordert.
The aim of this report is ...	Ziel dieses Berichts ist es, das Produkt ...
to compare / to review / to examine / to contrast / to recommend this product.	... zu vergleichen / zu überprüfen / zu untersuchen / gegenüberzustellen / zu empfehlen.
Our findings are as follows ...	Unsere Ergebnisse sind wie folgt ...
We found that ...	Wir sind der Auffassung, dass ...
It is clear from these findings that ...	Aus diesen Ergebnissen wird deutlich, dass ...
The best-selling/last-successful product is ...	Das meistgekaufte / am wenigsten erfolgreiche Produkt ist ...
Perhaps this is because of ...	Das liegt vielleicht an ...
The most common suggestion for improvement was ...	Der häufigste Verbesserungsvorschlag war ...
Based on the above findings we recommend ...	Basierend auf den obigen Ergebnissen empfehlen wir ...
In the light of these things we suggest ...	Angesichts dieser Tatsachen schlagen wir ... vor.

UNIT 8, Extra practice

3	matching	['mætʃɪŋ]	passend
	accessory	[ək'sesəri]	Zubehör, Accessoire
	abuse	[ə'bjuːs]	Missbrauch
	permalink	['pɜːməlɪŋk]	Permalink
7	relief	[rɪ'liːf]	Erleichterung
8	significant	[sɪg'nɪfɪkənt]	bedeutend, erheblich
	whether	['weðə]	ob
cs	etiquette	['etɪket]	Etikette, Kodex
	relationship-building	[rɪ'leɪʃnʃɪp bɪldɪŋ]	beziehungsstärkend
	to strike	[straɪk]	aufschlagen, auftreffen
	to strike the right tone	[straɪk ðə ˌraɪt 'təʊn]	den richtigen Ton treffen
	to the point	[tə ðə 'pɔɪnt]	kurz, präzise
	demand	[dɪ'mɑːnd]	Forderung

UNIT 9, Part A

▶	training programme	['treɪnɪŋ prəʊgræm]	Mitarbeitertraining, Schulungsprogramm
1	to revolutionize	[ˌrevə'luːʃənaɪz]	revolutionieren, grundlegend verändern
	cross-cultural	[ˌkrɒs'kʌltʃərəl]	interkulturell

relocation	[ˌriːləʊ'keɪʃn]	Standortwechsel, Versetzung
consulting	[kən'sʌltɪŋ]	Beratung
assignment	[ə'saɪnmənt]	Aufgabe, Auftrag
smooth	[smuːð]	reibungslos, problemlos
transfer	['trænsfɜː]	Versetzung, Transfer, Wechsel
competitive	[kəm'petətɪv]	wettbewerbsorientiert, konkurrenzfähig
presence	['prezns]	Präsenz, Anwesenheit
root	[ruːt]	Wurzel, Stamm
on site	[ɒn 'saɪt]	vor Ort
true to	['truː tə]	getreu
diversity	[daɪ'vɜːsəti]	Vielfalt, Verschiedenheit

3	subscriber	[səb'skraɪbə]	Abonnent/in, Empfänger/in
	decade	['dekeɪd]	Jahrzehnt
	president	['prezɪdənt]	Präsident/in, Vorsitzende/r
	overseas	[ˌəʊvə'siːz]	Auslands-, ausländisch
	business practice	['bɪznəs præktɪs]	Geschäftspraxis
5	takeover	['teɪkəʊvə]	Übernahme
	concerned	[kən'sɜːnd]	besorgt
	only	['əʊnli]	erst
	worried	['wʌrid]	besorgt, beunruhigt
6	to forward	['fɔːwəd]	schicken, nachsenden
	to google	['guːgl]	googeln
	brother-in-law	['brʌðər ɪn lɔː]	Schwager
	specialty	['speʃəlti]	Spezialität
7	to be stuck	[bi 'stʌk]	stecken bleiben, festsitzen
2.28	delayed	[dɪ'leɪd]	verspätet
	to get to know	[get tə 'nəʊ]	kennenlernen

UNIT 9, Part B

1	to invite sb out for a meal	[ɪnvaɪt ˌaʊt fər ə 'miːl]	jmdn zum Essen einladen
2.29	Here's to ... !	['hɪəz tə]	Auf ein/e ... !
	partnership	['pɑːtnəʃɪp]	Zusammenarbeit, Partnerschaft
	Cheers!	[tʃɪəz]	Prost!
	wheat	[wiːt]	Weizen
	highlight	['haɪlaɪt]	Höhepunkt
	ever since	[ˌevə 'sɪns]	seitdem
	rumour	['ruːmə]	Gerücht
	heart	[hɑːt]	Herz, Kern
	dramatic	[drə'mætɪk]	dramatisch
	to take things slowly	[teɪk ˌθɪŋz 'sləʊli]	Dinge langsam angehen
	early on	[ɜːli 'ɒn]	sehr früh, sehr bald

to subscribe	[səb'skraɪb]	abonnieren, beziehen
to get across	[ˌget ə'krɒs]	vermitteln
humorous	['hju:mərəs]	humorvoll, witzig
buffet	['bʊfeɪ]	Büffet
server	['sɜːvə]	Kellner
to fill up	[ˌfɪl 'ʌp]	auffüllen
delicacy	['delɪkəsi]	Delikatesse
liverwurst	['lɪvəwɜːst]	Leberwurst
conservative	[kən'sɜːvətɪv]	konservativ
anyway	['eniweɪ]	wie dem auch sei, also
2 impatient	[ɪm'peɪʃnt]	ungeduldig
irritated	['ɪrɪteɪtɪd]	gereizt
3 cap	[kæp]	Mütze, Kappe
pea	[pi:]	Erbse
to spy	[spaɪ]	spionieren
to bill sb	[bɪl]	jmdm die Rechnung schicken
4 snack	[snæk]	Snack
side dish	['saɪd dɪʃ]	Beilage
sweet	[swi:t]	Süßigkeit, Nachspeise
beef	[bi:f]	Rindfleisch
pork	[pɔ:k]	Schweinefleisch
veal	[vi:l]	Kalbfleisch
sausage	['sɒsɪdʒ]	Wurst
dumpling	['dʌmplɪŋ]	Kloß, Knödel
sauce	[sɔ:s]	Soße
to fry	[fraɪ]	*(in der Pfanne)* braten, frittieren
to roast	[rəʊst]	*(im Ofen)* braten, rösten, schmoren
to boil	[bɔɪl]	kochen, sieden
to bake	[beɪk]	backen
oven	['ʌvn]	Ofen
salty	['sɔ:lti]	salzig
sweet	[swi:t]	süß
heavy	['hevi]	mächtig, schwer
to cook	[kʊk]	kochen
house style	['haʊs staɪl]	nach Art des Hauses
5 to host	[həʊst]	ausrichten, veranstalten
to serve	[sɜːv]	servieren
favourite	['feɪvərɪt]	Lieblings-
grilled	[grɪld]	gegrillt
breast	[brest]	Brust
to top	[tɒp]	*hier:* überziehen, garnieren
creamy	['kri:mi]	cremig, sahnig
garlic	['gɑ:lɪk]	Knoblauch

	mushroom	['mʌʃrʊm]	Pilz
	to whip	[wɪp]	schlagen
	whipped cream	['wɪpt kriːm]	Schlagsahne
6	plenty of	['plenti əv]	reichlich
	to make fun of sb	[meɪk 'fʌn əv]	sich über jmdn lustig machen
7	joke	[dʒəʊk]	Witz
	sense of humour	[səns əv 'hjuːmə]	Sinn für Humor
	to force	[fɔːs]	zwingen

Giving advice

As far as … is concerned, it's important to …	Was … betrifft, ist es wichtig …
If you want …, you had better (not) …	Wenn Sie … wollen, hätten Sie besser (nicht) …
You don't have to …, but you probably should …	Sie müssen nicht …, aber vielleicht sollten Sie …
Most people here expect …	Die meisten Leute hier erwarten …
More and more business people …	Immer mehr Geschäftsleute …
It's hard to generalize, but it's usually better to …	Es ist schwierig zu verallgemeinern, aber normalerweise ist es besser …

8	mobile home	[ˌməʊbaɪl 'həʊm]	Wohnmobil
	perfume	['pɜːfjuːm]	Parfum
	sweetness	['swiːtnəs]	Süße
	to globalize	['gləʊbəlaɪz]	globalisieren
	beauty	['bjuːti]	Schönheit
	advancement	[əd'vɑːnsmənt]	Fortschritt
	to downplay	['daʊnpleɪ]	herunterspielen
	origin	['ɒrɪdʒɪn]	Ursprung, Herkunft
	mobility	[məʊ'bɪləti]	Mobilität, Beweglichkeit
9	to ensure	[ɪn'ʃʊə]	gewährleisten
	dress code	['dres kəʊd]	Kleiderordnung
	as far as	[əz 'fɑːr əz]	soweit wie

UNIT 9, Business file

1	sunrise	['sʌnraɪz]	Sonnenaufgang
	electromechanical	[ɪˌlektrəʊmɪ'kænɪkl]	elektromechanisch
2.31	consignment	[kən'saɪnmənt]	Sendung, Versendung
	platinum	['plætɪnəm]	Platin
	microchip	['maɪkrəʊtʃɪp]	Mikrochip
	to annoy	[ə'nɔɪ]	ärgern, stören
	enormous	[ɪ'nɔːməs]	riesig, ungeheuer groß

2	to **sympathize**	['sɪmpəθaɪz]	Verständnis haben
	to **take the blame**	[teɪk ðə 'bleɪm]	die Schuld auf sich nehmen

Making complaints

There seems to be a slight problem / *a bit of a problem.*	Es scheint ein kleines Problem zu geben.
I'm afraid we haven't received … yet.	Leider haben wir … noch nicht erhalten.
It looks like I was sent the wrong order.	Es sieht so aus, als hätte man mir die falsche Bestellung geschickt.
A number of items at the consignment were faulty/damaged/broken.	Eine Teil der Lieferung war fehlerhaft/ beschädigt/kaputt.
What do you want me to do with the consignment?	Was soll ich mit der Lieferung machen?
I'm very dissatisfied/unhappy with the service you provided.	Ich bin sehr unzufrieden mit Ihrem Service.
What kind of compensation can you offer us?	Was für eine Entschädigung können Sie uns anbieten?

3	**point of view**	[ˌpɔɪnt əv 'vjuː]	Standpunkt, Perspektive
	to **let off steam** *(coll.)*	[let ˌɒf 'stiːm]	Dampf ablassen
	white lie	[ˌwaɪt 'laɪ]	Notlüge
	to **protect**	[prə'tekt]	schützen
	award	[ə'wɔːd]	*hier:* Entschädigung
	honesty	['ɒnəsti]	Ehrlichkeit
4	**willingness**	['wɪlɪŋnəs]	Bereitschaft
	embarrassing	[ɪm'bærəsɪŋ]	peinlich
	to **role-play**	['rəʊl pleɪ]	ein Rollenspiel machen
	faulty	['fɔːlti]	fehlerhaft
	broken	['brəʊkən]	kaputt
	compensation	[ˌkɒmpen'seɪʃn]	Schadensersatz, Entschädigung
	to **hold sth up**	[ˌhəʊld 'ʌp]	etw verzögern, aufhalten

What's the problem exactly?	Was genau ist das Problem?
Oh dear, I'm sorry to hear that.	Oh je, das tut mir leid.
Do you have an order number /	Haben Sie eine Bestellnummer /
invoice number for me?	Rechnungsnummer für mich?
Obviously, something has gone wrong here.	Hier lief offensichtlich etwas schief.
I'm afraid the delivery has been held up a bit.	Leider verzögert sich die Lieferung etwas.
The order hasn't been processed yet.	Die Bestellung wurde noch nicht bearbeitet.
I'll deal with this straight away.	Ich werde das gleich erledigen.
I'll sort this out for you immediately.	Ich werde das sofort für Sie klären.
I'll look into it now and call you back.	Ich werde das jetzt überprüfen und Sie zurückrufen.

UNIT 9, Extra practice

1	tyre	['taɪə]	Reifen
3	franchise	['fræntʃaɪz]	Franchise, Lizenz
	resource centre	[rɪ'sɔːs sentə]	Informationszentrum
	cosmetic	[kɒz'metɪk]	Kosmetik
	to compete	[kəm'piːt]	konkurrieren
4	to carry on	[ˌkæri 'ɒn]	weitermachen
6	vegetable	['vedʒtəbl]	Gemüse
CS	tab	[tæb]	Rechnung
	to buy a round	[baɪ ə 'raʊnd]	eine Runde ausgeben
	to go Dutch *(coll.)*	[gəʊ 'dʌtʃ]	getrennt bezahlen
	to treat sb to sth	[triːt]	jmdn zu etw einladen
	to turn down	[ˌtɜːn 'daʊn]	ablehnen
	engagement	[ɪn'geɪdʒmənt]	Verpflichtung
	to be tied up	[bi ˌtaɪd 'ʌp]	(dienstlich) verhindert sein
	to give a rain check *(coll.)*	[gɪv ə 'reɪn tʃek]	auf eine Einladung ein anderes Mal zurückkommen

to turn down an invitation	eine Einladung ablehnen
Perhaps another time?	Vielleicht ein anderes Mal?
Unfortunately I have another engagement.	Leider habe ich eine anderweitige Verpflichtung.
I'm afraid I'm tied up.	Ich bin leider verhindert.
I hope you'll give me a rain check.	Ich hoffe, wir können die Einladung ein anderes Mal wahrmachen.

UNIT 10, Part A

►	to lock	[lɒk]	zuschließen, abschließen
	hypothetical	[ˌhaɪpə'θetɪkl]	hypothetisch
	to pitch	[pɪtʃ]	*hier:* anbieten
1	peripheral	[pə'rɪfərəl]	nebensächlich, Rand-
	digital	['dɪdʒɪtl]	digital
	tier	[tɪə]	Ebene, Rang, Stufe
	tier one supplier	[tɪə 'wʌn səplaɪə]	Lieferant der ersten Ebene
	personalized	['pɜːsənəlaɪzd]	personalisiert, individuell gestaltet
	camera	['kæmərə]	Kamera
	user	['juːzə]	Nutzer/in
	touch screen	['tʌtʃ skriːn]	Touchscreen, Berührungsbildschirm
	to take pictures	[teɪk 'pɪktʃəz]	Fotos machen
	secondary	['sekəndri]	zweitrangig, sekundär
2	proposition	[ˌprɒpə'zɪʃn]	Vorschlag, Angebot
	short-term	[ˌʃɔːt'tɜːm]	kurzfristig
	seasonal	['siːzənl]	Saison-, jahreszeitlich
	storage	['stɔːrɪdʒ]	Lagerung, *Computer:* Speicherung
	to customize	['kʌstəmaɪz]	individuell gestalten
3	just-in-time	[ˌdʒʌst ɪn 'taɪm]	*hier:* bedarfsorientiert
2.33	inventory	['ɪnvəntri]	Inventar, Warenbestand
	to assemble	[ə'sembl]	montieren, zusammenbauen
	personalization	[ˌpɜːsənəlaɪ'zeɪʃn]	Personalisierung
	efficient	[ɪ'fɪʃnt]	effizient
	constant	['kɒnstənt]	dauernd, ständig
	aware of sth	[ə'weər əv]	einer Sache bewusst
	to run low	[ˌrʌn 'ləʊ]	sinken, zur Neige gehen
	mainland	['meɪnlænd]	Festland
	identification	[aɪˌdentɪfɪ'keɪʃn]	Identifikation
	barcode	['bɑːkəʊd]	Strichkode
	to scan	[skæn]	scannen
	to link	[lɪŋk]	verlinken, verbinden
6	copycat	['kɒpikæt]	Nachahmer/in, Kopierer/in
	variation	[ˌveəri'eɪʃn]	Variante, Variation
	asset	['æset]	Vermögen
	appreciation	[əˌpriːʃi'eɪʃn]	*hier:* Wertsteigerung
	depreciation	[dɪˌpriːʃi'eɪʃn]	Wertminderung, Wertverlust
	growth	[grəʊθ]	Wachstum

UNIT 10, Part B

1	analyst	['ænəlɪst]	Experte/Expertin
	cutback	['kʌtbæk]	Kürzung
2	to affect	[ə'fekt]	betreffen, sich auswirken
2.34	to speed up	[ˌspiːd 'ʌp]	beschleunigen
	attack	[ə'tæk]	Angriff
	to approve	[ə'pruːv]	genehmigen, einverstanden sein
	unreasonable	[ʌn'riːznəbl]	unvernünftig
	to aim high	[ˌeɪm 'haɪ]	sich hohe Ziele setzen
	to implement	['ɪmplɪment]	umsetzen, einführen
	to afford sth	[ə'fɔːd]	sich etw leisten
	to lease	[liːs]	mieten, leasen
	to trust	[trʌst]	vertrauen
	strength	[streŋθ]	Stärke, Kraft
	weakness	['wiːknəs]	Schwäche
	threat	[θret]	Gefahr
4	unless	[ən'les]	wenn nicht, es sei denn
	to overestimate	[ˌəʊvər'estɪmeɪt]	überschätzen
	to extend	[ɪk'stend]	ausdehnen, verlängern
5	to relate	[rɪ'leɪt]	in Zusammenhang bringen
7	to deny	[dɪ'naɪ]	leugnen, verweigern, ablehnen
	to spare	[speə]	entbehren
	picnic	['pɪknɪk]	Picknick
	disappointed	[ˌdɪsə'pɔɪntɪd]	enttäuscht
8	to argue	['ɑːgjuː]	argumentieren, behaupten

Budget talk

Where do we go from here?	Wie soll es weitergehen?
It's as simple as that.	So einfach ist das.
Look at the longterm benefits / *the longterm sustainability of it.*	Schauen Sie sich die langfristigen Vorteile an.
We should see it as an investment.	Wir sollten es als Investition sehen.
We're really operating under a tight budget.	Wir haben wirklich (nur) ein knappes Budget zur Verfügung.
You think this is really necessary, do you?	Sie halten das wirklich für notwendig, oder?
I can't approve such a high budget increase.	Ich kann einer solchen Budget-Erhöhung nicht zustimmen.
We also need a back-up plan to minimize *our risk, just in case.*	Wir brauchen für alle Fälle einen Plan B, um unser Risiko zu verkleinern.

9	car stereo	['kɑː steriəʊ]	Autoradio
2.35	to commute	[kə'mjuːt]	pendeln
	commute	[kə'mjuːt]	Fahrt zur Arbeit, Pendelzeit
	treasure	['treʒə]	Schatz
	hunt	[hʌnt]	Jagd, Suche
	translator	[træns'leɪtə]	Übersetzer/in
	accent	['æksent]	Akzent
10	spare time	[ˌspeə 'taɪm]	Freizeit

UNIT 10, Business file

2.36	1	halfway	[ˌhɑːf'weɪ]	halbwegs, halb, auf halbem Weg
2.37		computing speed	[kəm'pjuːtɪŋ spiːd]	Rechnergeschwindigkeit
		input terminal	['ɪnpʊt tɜːmɪnl]	Eingabeterminal
		productivity	[ˌprɒdʌk'tɪvəti]	Produktivität, Leistung
		efficiency	[ɪ'fɪʃnsi]	Leistungsfähigkeit, Effizienz
		to disappear	[ˌdɪsə'pɪə]	verschwinden
2.38		to bring sb up to date	[brɪŋ ˌʌp tə 'deɪt]	jmdn auf den neuesten Stand bringen
		to build on sth	['bɪld ɒn]	auf etw aufbauen
		to be left over	[bi ˌleft 'əʊvə]	übrig sein
	4	savings	['seɪvɪŋz]	Ersparnisse
		funding	['fʌndɪŋ]	Gelder, Mittel, Finanzierung
		downside	['daʊnsaɪd]	Kehrseite, Nachteil

UNIT 10, Extra practice

5	to lead	[liːd]	führen
	death	[deθ]	Tod
6	to gain	[geɪn]	gewinnen
9	sufficient	[sə'fɪʃnt]	genügend
CS	judgement	['dʒʌdʒmənt]	Urteilsvermögen, Meinung
	eye	[aɪ]	Auge
	hug	[hʌg]	Umarmung
	to give sb a wave	[gɪv ə 'weɪv]	jmdm zuwinken
	sincere	[sɪn'sɪə]	aufrichtig, ehrlich
	to strengthen	['streŋθn]	stärken, verstärken

BUSINESS CORRESPONDENCE

1	block style	['blɒk staɪl]	Blocksatz
	font	[fɒnt]	Schrift
	to fulfill	[fʊl'fɪl]	erfüllen
	to accompany	[ə'kʌmpəni]	beifügen

	literature	['lɪtrətʃə]	*hier:* Prospekte
2	to vary	['veəri]	variieren, sich ändern
	theme	[θiːm]	Thema
	venue	['venjuː]	Veranstaltungsort
	to reimburse	[ˌriːɪm'bɜːs]	entschädigen
	in due course	[ɪn ˌdjuː 'kɔːs]	zu gegebener Zeit, zur rechten Zeit
	close	[kləʊz]	Abschluss, Briefschluss
3	chamber of commerce	[ˌtʃeɪmbə əv 'kɒmɜːs]	Industrie- und Handelskammer
	aerospace	['eərəʊspeɪs]	Luft- und Raumfahrt
	to obtain	[əb'teɪn]	erhalten
	trade directory	[ˌtreɪd də'rektəri]	Branchenadressbuch
4	to hesitate	['hezɪteɪt]	zögern
5	impressed	[ɪm'prest]	beeindruckt
	hint	[hɪnt]	Anspielung
	satisfactory	[ˌsætɪs'fæktəri]	ausreichend, befriedigend
6	to dispatch	[dɪ'spætʃ]	abfertigen, abschicken
7	recruitment agency	[rɪ'kruːtmənt eɪdʒənsi]	Arbeitsvermittlung
	proud(ly)	[praʊd]	stolz
	farewell	[ˌfeə'wel]	Abschied
	valued	['væljuːd]	geschätzt, gewürdigt
8	subtitle	['sʌbtaɪtl]	Untertitel
	essential	[ɪ'senʃl]	äußerst wichtig, entscheidend
	enthusiastic	[ɪnˌθjuːzi'æstɪk]	enthusiastisch, begeistert
10	punctuation	[ˌpʌŋktʃu'eɪʃn]	Zeichensetzung, Interpunktion
	limitation	[ˌlɪmɪ'teɪʃn]	Begrenzung, Beschränkung

A

abbreviation **5 B** Abkürzung

ability **2 A** Fähigkeit

able: to be ~ to do sth **WU** etw tun können

about: to care ~ sth **5 A** sich um etw sorgen, kümmern

abrupt **3 EP** schroff, brüsk

abuse **8 EP** Missbrauch

academic **2 A** Schul-, wissenschaftlich, akademisch

accent **10 B** Akzent

acceptable **5 A** akzeptabel

to access **3 B** erreichen

accessory **8 EP** Zubehör, Accessoire

accommodation **2 B** Unterkunft, Zimmer

to accompany **BC** beifügen

according to **1 B** zufolge, laut, nach, entsprechend

accordingly **2 BF** dementsprechend, folglich

account **6 EP** Bericht; to take into ~ **8 BF** berücksichtigen

to accuse **2 EP** anklagen

acquaintance **7 A** der/die Bekannte

to acquire **7 A** erwerben

acronym **5 EP** Abkürzung, Kurzwort

across: to come ~ **3 EP** (auf andere) wirken; to get ~ **9 B** vermitteln

to act out **7 A** durchspielen

action **3 A** Handlung

activity: business ~ **1 B** Geschäftsaktivität

actual **2 B** wirklich

ad (abbr.: advertisement) **3 A** Anzeige

to adapt **3 A** anpassen

adaptable **6 A** anpassungsfähig, flexibel

addition **6 A** Bereicherung, Ergänzung

additional **5 A** zusätzlich

adhesive **1 B** Klebstoff

advanced **8 A** hochentwickelt, fortgeschritten

advancement **9 B** Fortschritt

advantage **7 B** Vorteil

adventurous **8 BF** abenteuerlustig

to advertise **5 A** ankündigen, zum Verkauf anbieten

advice **1 EP** Ratschlag

aeronautics **1 B** Flugtechnik

aeroplane **1 B** Flugzeug

aerospace **BC** Luft- und Raumfahrt

to affect **10 B** betreffen, sich auswirken

affected **4 A** betroffen

to afford sth **10 B** sich etw leisten

afterwards **6 A** danach

against **5 BF** gegen

agency: recruitment ~ **BC** Arbeitsvermittlung

agent **1 A** hier: Bearbeiter/in, Mitarbeiter/in

agricultural **3 A** landwirtschaftlich

ahead: to go ~ **1 A** weitermachen; to look ~ **4 A** in die Zukunft blicken

aim **7 BF** Ziel, Absicht

to aim high **10 B** sich hohe Ziele setzen

all over **WU** überall

to allow for sth **7 BF** etw zulassen

all-round **8 BF** vielseitig, Allround-

alone **1 A** allein; stand-alone **8 B** alleinstehend, freistehend

Alpine **1 B** Alpen-, alpin

alternative **6 BF** alternativ

although **6 BF** obwohl

amusing **6 EP** lustig

analyst **10 B** Experte/Expertin

to annoy **9 BF** ärgern, stören

to anticipate **7 BF** erwarten, rechnen mit, vorhersehen

anymore **7 A** nicht mehr

anything else **4 BF** noch etwas

anyway **9 B** wie dem auch sei, also

apparently **4 EP** anscheinend, scheinbar

to **appeal** **8 A** gefallen, ansprechen

appearance **8 A** Erscheinungsbild

applicant **2 EP** Bewerber/in

appraisal **6 B** Beurteilung, Mitarbeiter-gespräch

to **appreciate** **3 B** dankbar sein

appreciation **10 A** *hier:* Wertsteigerung

appropriate **2 EP** angemessen, passend, geeignet

approval **5 A** Zustimmung

to **approve** **10 B** genehmigen, einverstanden sein

approximately **4 A** nahezu, fast

to **argue** **10 B** argumentieren, behaupten

to **arise** **4 B** entstehen, sich ergeben

around **8 A** *hier:* vorhanden, da; to **look** ~ **7 A** herumschauen; to **move** ~ **1 A** umherbewegen, transportieren

arrow **3 A** Pfeil

art **1 BF** Kunst

as: ~ **a matter of fact** **6 BF** in der Tat, tatsächlich; **as far as** **9 B** soweit wie; ~ **follows** **4 A** wie folgt; ~ **they say** **5 A** wie man sagt; **such** ~ **8 A** wie beispielsweise

asking price **5 A** geforderter Preis

asparagus **7 B** Spargel

to **assemble** **10 A** montieren, zusammenbauen

assembly line **3 B** Montageband

asset **10 A** Vermögen

assignment **9 A** Aufgabe, Auftrag

association **2 A** Kontakt, Verband

assortment **8 B** Auswahl

to **assume** **6 BF** annehmen, vermuten

at: ~ **first glance** **8 A** auf den ersten Blick; ~ **the end of the day** **8 A** letztendlich; ~ **the latest** **8 B** spätestens

to **attach** **3 B** befestigen

attack **10 B** Angriff

to **attempt** **3 B** versuchen

attendee **7 B** Teilnehmer/in, Anwesende/r

attention **7 BF** Aufmerksamkeit

to **attract** **8 A** anziehen, auf sich ziehen

audiobook **6 A** Hörbuch

automatic **7 B** automatisch

automotive **1 B** Automobil-, Kraftfahrzeug-

average **4 A** Durchschnitts-, durchschnittlich

to **avoid** **4 EP** vermeiden

award **9 BF** *hier:* Entschädigung

aware of sth **10 A** einer Sache bewusst

awareness **8 A** Bewusstsein

away: to **get** ~ **1 A** wegkommen, weg-gehen; **walk-away point** **5 A** Schmerzgrenze

awkward **7 EP** ungünstig

B

back **7 B** Hinterseite, Rückseite

back: ~ **in 2000** **6 A** damals, im Jahr 2000; to **be** ~ **on track** **7 B** wieder auf dem richtigen Weg sein; **back-up** **4 B** Reserve, Ersatz; to **pay** ~ **7 A** zurück-zahlen; to **read** ~ **1 BF** nochmal vorlesen

background **2 A** Hintergrund

to **bake** **9 B** backen

to **balance** **4 A** ausgleichen, aufwiegen

bandwidth **7 B** Bandbreite

bank: community ~ **1 BF** lokale/ unabhängige Bank

barcode **10 A** Strichcode

to **bargain** **5 A** verhandeln, handeln

bargain: to **drive a hard** ~ **5 A** hart verhandeln

barman **7 B** Barkeeper

base **6 B** *Baseball:* Mal, Base

based: be ~ **on sth** **4 A** auf etw basieren

basic **7 BF** grundlegend, wesentlich, Basis-

basically **1 B** im Grunde, im Prinzip

basis **1 A** Basis

bath **1 B** Bad

be: to ~ able to do sth **WU** etw tun können; **to ~ back on track** **7 B** wieder auf dem richtigen Weg sein; **~ based on sth** **4 A** auf etw basieren; **to ~ behind schedule** **2 A** im Verzug sein; **to ~ between jobs** **1 A** arbeitslos sein; **to ~ in for sth** **4 A** etw zu erwarten haben; **to ~ into sth** **5 B** sich für etw interessieren; **to ~ left over** **10 BF** übrig sein; **to ~ priced** **8 A** kosten; **to ~ set in stone** **4 A** unverrückbar sein; **to ~ stuck** **9 A** stecken bleiben, festsitzen; **to ~ tied up** **9 EP** dienstlich verhindert sein

to beat **4 EP** schlagen; **to ~ sb to the market** **5 EP** jmdn auf dem Markt/im Wettbewerb schlagen

beauty **9 B** Schönheit

beef **9 B** Rindfleisch

beforehand **3 EP** vorher, im Voraus

to begin **1 A** beginnen, starten

behind: to be ~ schedule **2 A** im Verzug sein

beige **3 A** beige

to believe **6 EP** glauben

belt **3 B** Gürtel, Band; **conveyor ~** **3 B** Fließband, Förderband

to benefit **5 A** profitieren

benefit **2 A** Nutzen, Vorteil

besides **8 A** außerdem

between: to be ~ jobs **1 A** arbeitslos sein

beyond **1 B** darüber hinaus

bill **7 B** Rechnung

to bill sb **9 B** jmdm die Rechnung schicken

biodegradable **8 A** biologisch abbaubar

bird **4 EP** Vogel

biscuit **3 A** Keks

blade **6 A** Klinge

blame **9 BF** Schuld; **to take the ~** **9 BF** die Schuld auf sich nehmen

to blame **4 EP** beschuldigen

blank **3 BF** leer, unbeschrieben

to block **4 B** blockieren, sperren

block: ~ style **BC** Blocksatz

to blow **7 B** blasen, wehen

bn = billion **4 A** Milliarde

body **1 B** Körper; **~ language** **7 BF** Körpersprache

to boil **9 B** kochen, sieden

bonus **2 B** Bonus, Prämie

book: e-book **2 B** elektronisches Buch

booked: double-booked **6 BF** *hier:* mehrfach verabredet

to borrow **7 A** sich leihen, sich borgen

bossy **EP** rechthaberisch

bottom **1 B** Grund, Boden

brand: ~ name **1 B** Markenname

break: to take a ~ **1 A** eine Pause machen

to break **4 A** brechen, verletzen

breakdown **5 BF** Aufschlüsselung

breast **9 B** Brust

briefly **6 B** kurz

to bring: to ~ out **4 A** herausbringen; **to ~ sb up to date** **10 BF** jmdn auf den neuesten Stand bringen; **to ~ sb up to speed** **4 A** jmdn auf den neuesten Stand bringen

broken **9 BF** kaputt

brother-in-law **9 A** Schwager

buffet **9 B** Buffet

to build: to ~ on sth **10 BF** auf etw aufbauen; **relationship-building** **8 EP** beziehungsstärkend

bulk **5 A** Menge, Masse

bureaucracy **2 A** Bürokratie

to burn out **5 B** ausbrennen, sich kaputt machen

business: ~ activity **1 B** Geschäftsaktivität; **~ partner** **WU** Geschäftspartner/in; **~ practice** **9 A** Geschäftspraxis; **~ unit** **1 B** Geschäftsbereich; **to get down to ~** **3 EP** zum Geschäftlichen übergehen; **to go out of ~** **8 B** Konkurs gehen

to **buy**: to ~ **a round** **9 EP** eine Runde
ausgeben

by: ~ **chance** **3 BF** zufällig; ~ **hand** **1 BF**
in Handarbeit; to **get** ~ **1 EP** zurechtkommen; to **stop** ~ **7 A** vorbeikommen

C

to **calculate** **7 B** berechnen, ausrechnen

call: ~ **centre** **1 A** Callcenter; to **return a**
~ **1 BF** zurückrufen

caller **2 BF** Anrufer/in

to **calm down** **4 B** sich beruhigen

camera **10 A** Kamera

cap **9 B** Mütze, Kappe

capital **7 A** Kapital

car stereo **10 B** Autoradio

care **1 A** Sorge, Betreuung; **hair-care**
1 B Haarpflege

to **care**: to ~ **about sth** **5 A** sich um etw
sorgen, kümmern

career: **careers fair** **1 B** Firmenmesse,
Jobbörse

to **carry on** **9 EP** weitermachen

to **catch** **1 BF** *hier*: verstehen, mitbe-
kommen; **3 B** *hier*: erwischen,
erreichen; to ~ **up** **1 BF** *hier*: treffen

to **cause** **4 A** verursachen

to **celebrate** **5 EP** feiern

centre: **call** ~ **1 A** Callcenter

CEO = Chief Executive Officer **1 A**
Geschäftsführer/in, Vorstandschef/in

certain **7 A** gewiss, bestimmt

CFO = Chief Financial Officer **1 A**
Finanzchef/in, Leiter/in der
Finanzabteilung

to **chair** **4 A** den Vorsitz haben, leiten

challenge **2 B** Herausforderung

challenging **6 A** herausfordernd

chamber of commerce **BC** Industrie- und
Handelskammer

champagne **5 EP** Champagner, Sekt

chance **2 A** Gelegenheit, Chance; **by** ~
3 BF zufällig

to **change**: to ~ **your mind** **5 BF** es sich
anders überlegen

changeover **4 B** Übergang, Umstellung

character **WU** Figur, Person

Chardonnay **1 BF** Chardonnay

chat **1 A** Plausch, kurze Unterhaltung

check: to **give a rain** ~ **9 EP** auf eine
Einladung ein anderes Mal zurückkommen

Cheers! **9 B** Prost!

cheque **5 BF** Scheck

to **chew** **6 B** kauen

Chianti **7 B** Chianti

chin **6 EP** Kinn

choice **5 BF** Wahl, Entscheidung

to **choose** **1 BF** wählen

to **chop** **6 B** hacken, klein schneiden

CIO = Chief Information Officer **1 A**
Leiter/in der Abteilung Informations-
technologie

civil **1 A** Bürger-, Staats-; ~ **service** **1 A**
Behörde, öffentlicher Dienst

classic **8 BF** klassisch

to **clean** **WU** putzen, säubern; **cleaning**
product **WU** Putzmittel

to **clear** **7 B** *hier*: abräumen

clerk **1 A** Büroangestellte/r

close **BC** Abschluss, Briefschluss

close **3 B** dicht, nah

closely **1 A** eng, dicht

closing **3 A** Schluss

clue **WU** Hinweis, Tipp

COD = cash on delivery **5 BF** Barzahlung
bei Lieferung

code: **dress** ~ **9 B** Kleiderordnung

collage **3 BF** Collage

to **collocate** **5 EP** kollokieren,
zusammenstellen

collocation **1 A** Kollokation

colloquial **8 B** umgangssprachlich

column **2 A** Spalte

combination **2 A** Kombination,
Verbindung

to **come:** to ~ **across** **3 EP** (auf andere)
wirken; to ~ **on the market** **WU** auf
den Markt kommen; to ~ **up** **6 BF**
dazwischenkommen; to ~ **your way**
2 B einem über den Weg laufen

comment **8 B** Kommentar

commerce: chamber of ~ **BC** Industrie-
und Handelskammer

commercial **1 BF** Werbesport

commitment **5 A** Einsatz, Engagement

common **WU** gemeinsam, allgemein; to
have sth in ~ **with sb** **WU** etw mit
jmdm gemeinsam haben

to **communicate** **7 B** kommunizieren

community: ~ **bank** **1 BF** lokale/
unabhängige Bank

commute **10 B** Fahrt zur Arbeit,
Pendelzeit

to **commute** **10 B** pendeln

commuter **3 A** Pendler/in

company: Ltd = Limited Company *(BrE)*
1 B GmbH; **parent** ~ **1 B** Muttergesellschaft; **plc = Public Limited** ~
(BrE) **1 B** AG; to **run a** ~ **WU** ein
Geschäft führen, betreiben

comparison **5 A** Vergleich

compensation **9 BF** Schadensersatz,
Entschädigung

competing **9 EP** konkurrieren

competitive **9 A** wettbewerbsorientiert,
konkurrenzfähig

to **complain** **4 EP** sich beschweren

complete **2 A** komplett, vollständig

completely **1 BF** völlig, absolut, total

complex **8 B** komplex, kompliziert

compliment **3 BF** Kompliment

component **2 A** Bestandteil, Komponente

computing speed **10 BF** Rechner-
geschwindigkeit

concentrate **8 B** Konzentrat

to **concentrate** **5 B** sich konzentrieren

concept **4 A** Konzept

concern **4 B** Bedenken, Besorgnis

concerned **9 A** besorgt

conclusion **8 A** Schlussfolgerung

concrete **1 BF** konkret

to **conduct** **7 B** führen

to **confuse** **6 B** durcheinanderbringen

confused **5 A** verwirrt

to **connect with sb** **1 EP** mit jmdm in
Verbindung treten

consequence **8 A** Konsequenz, Folge

consequently **8 A** folglich, deshalb

conservative **9 B** konservativ

to **consider** **2 EP** halten für, ansehen als

consignment **9 BF** Sendung, Versendung

constant **10 A** dauernd, ständig

to **construct** **1 B** bauen, errichten

consulting **9 A** Beratung

container **8 A** Behälter, Gefäß

context **2 A** Zusammenhang, Kontext

continent **1 B** Kontinent

contractor **3 A** Vertragspartner/in

to **contrast** **8 BF** vergleichen, gegenüber-
stellen

conveyor belt **3 B** Fließband, Förderband

to **convince** **6 B** überzeugen

COO = Chief Operating Officer **1 A**
Betriebsleiter/in

to **cook** **9 B** kochen

cooperative **4 A** Genossenschaft

copycat **10 A** Nachahmer/in, Kopierer/in

core **2 B** Kern

corporate: ~ **culture** **1 B** Unternehmenskultur

**Corporation: Inc./Corp. = Incorporated
Closed** ~ *(AmE)* **1 B** GmbH

corridor **1 A** Flur, Korridor

cosmetic **9 EP** Kosmetik

cost: handling costs **4 B** Abwicklungskosten, Bearbeitungskosten

cotton **8 A** Baumwolle

council **2 B** Rat

counter **8 B** Tresen, Schalter

counterproductive **5 B** kontraproduktiv

couple **7 BF** Paar; **a ~ of** **2 B** einige, (ein) paar

cream: hand ~ **1 B** Handcreme

creamy **9 B** cremig, sahnig

to **criticize** **2 B** kritisieren

CRO = Chief Risk Officer **1 A** Risikomanager/in

to **cross:** **6 A** kreuzen; to **~ out** **6 A** streichen; to **keep one's fingers crossed** **6 B** die Daumen drücken

cross-cultural **9 A** interkulturell

crowd **1 BF** Menge, Masse

CTO = Chief Technology Officer **1 A** Technische Direktorin / Technischer Direktor

cultural **2 EP** kulturell; **cross-cultural** **9 A** interkulturell

culture: corporate ~ **1 B** Unternehmenskultur

cupcake **1 BF** kleiner Rührkuchen

customer: ~ base **1 B** Kundenbestand, Kundenstamm, Kundschaft; **~ care** **1 A** Kundendienst, Kundenbetreuung

to **customize** **10 A** individuell gestalten

to **cut** **8 A** *hier:* kürzen, senken; **~ off** **2 BF** abgeschnitten; to **~ out** **3 B** ausschneiden

cutback **10 B** Kürzung

cutlery **7 B** Besteck

to **cycle** **3 A** Rad fahren

cycling **2 A** Radfahren

D

daily **1 A** täglich

dairy **WU** Molkerei-, Milch-; **~ product** **WU** Milchprodukt

date: to bring sb up to ~ **10 BF** jmdn auf den neuesten Stand bringen

day: at the end of the ~ **8 A** letztendlich; **these days** **1 BF** heutzutage

damaged **3 B** beschädigt

death **10 EP** Tod

decade **9 A** Jahrzehnt

decaf (*abbr.:* **decaffeinated**) **1 A** koffeinfrei

to **decorate** **1 BF** dekorieren, schmücken, verzieren

defect **3 B** Fehler, Defekt

to **define** **4 A** definieren

definition **3 A** Definition

to **delay** **6 EP** aufhalten, verzögern

delayed **9 A** verspätet

to **delegate** **2 B** delegieren, beauftragen

delicacy **9 B** Delikatesse

delicious **1 BF** köstlich

delighted **3 BF** erfreut, entzückt

delivery: COD = cash on ~ **5 BF** Barzahlung bei Lieferung; **home ~** **1 BF** Hauszustellung

demand **8 EP** Forderung

demo **6 B** Vorführung

dentist **1 A** Zahnarzt, Zahnärztin

to **deny** **10 B** leugnen, verweigern, ablehnen

depreciation **10 A** Wertminderung, Wertverlust

deputy **1 A** Stellvertreter/in

designated **3 B** gekennzeichnet

desk: hot-desking **2 B** Arbeitsplatzwahl nach Verfügbarkeit

despite **8 A** trotz

detergent **8 A** Waschmittel, Spülmittel

diamond **6 A** Diamant

diary **1 A** (Termin-)Kalender

digital **10 A** digital

direct report **1 A** direkte Untergebene/r

directly **1 A** direkt, unmittelbar

disadvantage **7 B** Nachteil

to **disappear** **10 BF** verschwinden

disappointed **10 B** enttäuscht

disappointing **7 A** enttäuschend

to **discontinue** **8 BF** abbrechen, einstellen

to **discover** **3 BF** entdecken

discrimination **2 EP** Diskriminierung

dish **7 B** Gericht; **side ~** **9 B** Beilage

to **dispatch** **BC** abfertigen, abschicken

distribution **1 A** Vertrieb

district **3 BF** Bezirk, Gebiet, Viertel

to disturb **1 A** stören

diverse **1 B** unterschiedlich, vielfältig

diversity **9 A** Vielfalt, Verschiedenheit

divided **1 B** aufgeteilt

division **1 B** Abteilung

to do: Do you mind if ...? **1 A** Stört es Sie/dich, wenn ...?; to be able to ~ sth WU etw tun können; to get to ~ (sth) **1 BF** die Möglichkeit haben, etw zu tun

doctor **1 A** Arzt, Ärztin

double-booked **6 BF** *hier:* mehrfach verabredet

doubt **1 EP** Zweifel, Ungewissheit

down: to calm ~ **4 B** sich beruhigen; to get ~ to business **3 EP** zum Geschäftlichen übergehen; to sit ~ **1 A** sich hinsetzen

to download **2 B** herunterladen

to downplay **9 B** herunterspielen

downside **10 BF** Kehrseite, Nachteil

dramatic **9 B** dramatisch

dramatically **2 B** dramatisch

draught **7 B** Luftzug

to draw: to ~ sb's attention to sth **7 BF** jmds Aufmerksamkeit auf etw lenken; to ~ up **1 A** *hier:* entwerfen

drawback **8 A** Nachteil, Haken

dress: ~ code **9 B** Kleiderordnung

drill **3 B** Übung; **6 A** Bohrer

to drive: to ~ a hard bargain **5 A** hart verhandeln

driven **2 A** angetrieben

drug record **1 EP** Medikamentenregister/ -verzeichnis

drum **8 B** Trommel, Fass

due **4 BF** fällig; ~ to sth **4 A** aufgrund von etw

dumpling **9 B** Kloß, Knödel

during **1 A** während

Dutch **9 EP** holländisch, niederländisch; to go ~ *(coll.)* **9 EP** getrennt bezahlen

duty **1 A** Pflicht

E

eager **6 A** begierig, lernfreudig

early on **9 B** sehr früh, sehr bald

earplug **3 B** Ohrstöpsel

east **1 A** ost-, östlich

to eat out **4 A** essen gehen

e-book **2 B** elektronisches Buch

e-business **1 B** Internetgeschäft, -firma

echo **2 EP** Echo

eco **8 A** Öko-, Umwelt-

economical **2 A** sparsam

economy **5 B** Wirtschaft

edge **6 A** *hier:* Vorteil, Vorsprung

editor **6 A** Herausgeber/in

educational **2 A** Lern-, Ausbildungs-, Bildungs-

effective **5 B** wirksam, effektiv

efficiency **10 BF** Leistungsfähigkeit, Effizienz

efficient **10 A** effizient

either ... or ... **1 A** entweder ... oder ...

electric **8 BF** Elektro-, elektrisch

electromechanical **9 BF** elektromechanisch

elegant **3 A** elegant

else: anything ~ **4 BF** noch etwas

embarrassing **9 BF** peinlich

emergency **3 B** Notfall

employer **2 EP** Arbeitgeber/in

to encounter sth **8 BF** auf etw stoßen

to encourage **2 B** fördern

to end **2 BF** beenden

end: at the ~ of the day **8 A** letztendlich

energy bar **3 BF** Energie-Riegel

engagement **9 EP** Verpflichtung

engineer: safety ~ **1 A** Sicherheitsingenieur/in, Sicherheitstechniker/in

enjoyable **5 B** angenehm, unterhaltsam

enormous **9 BF** riesig, ungeheuer groß

enough **1 EP** genug

to **enquire** **8 B** untersuchen, sich
erkundigen

to **ensure** **9 B** gewährleisten

enthusiast **5 BF** *hier:* Fan, Anhänger/in

enthusiastic **BC** enthusiastisch, begeistert

entire **5 A** ganze/r/s

entry **7 A** Eintritt

environmentally **1 B** umwelt-;
environmentally-friendly **1 B** um-
weltfreundlich

equipment: lighting ~ **8 A** Lichtausrüstung

especially **1 B** besonders, vor allem

essential **BC** äußerst wichtig,
entscheidend

established: long-established **1 B** alteingeführt, alteingesessen

estate **1 BF** Besitz, Wohnsiedlung, (Land-)
Gut; **~ agency** **1 BF** Immobilienbüro

e-tail **1 A** Onlineversand-, Onlinehandel-

ethnic **2 A** ethnisch

etiquette **8 EP** Etikette, Kodex

ever since **9 B** seitdem

exaggerated **5 EP** übertrieben

to **examine** **8 BF** untersuchen

exception **4 BF** Ausnahme

exit **3 B** Ausgang

exotic **6 EP** exotisch

to **expand** **1 EP** expandieren, vergrößern

to **expect** **2 B** erwarten

expense **7 BF** (Geld-)Ausgabe

experienced **3 EP** erfahren

expertise **2 B** Fachwissen, Sachverstand

explanation **6 EP** Erklärung

to **export** **WU** exportieren

to **extend** **10 B** ausdehnen, verlängern

extensive **6 EP** umfassend

ex-works **5 BF** ab Werk

eye **10 EP** Auge

F

fabulous **3 BF** fabelhaft

to **face sth** **4 A** mit etw konfrontiert
werden

face to face **WU** von Angesicht zu
Angesicht

fact: as a matter of ~ **6 BF** in der Tat,
tatsächlich; **in ~** **1 A** um genau zu sein,
eigentlich

factfile **4 A** Steckbrief

factor **1 BF** Faktor

to **fail** **5 A** scheitern, missglücken

fair **4 A** gerecht

fair: careers ~ **1 B** Firmenmesse, Jobbörse

familiar with sth **1 B** mit etw vertraut

famous for **4 A** berühmt für

far: as ~ as **9 B** soweit wie

farewell **BC** Abschied

farm **1 BF** Bauernhof, Farm

farmer **4 A** Landwirt/in

fashion **1 A** Mode; **old-fashioned** **1 BF**
altmodisch

fault **5 BF** Fehler, Schuld

faulty **9 BF** fehlerhaft

favour **3 A** Gefallen

favourite **9 B** Lieblings-

feasible **5 A** machbar, möglich

to **feature sb** **6 A** jmdn in einer Hauptrolle
haben

fee **5 BF** Gebühr

feminine **8 BF** weiblich, feminin

few **2 A** wenige

field **1 BF** Gebiet, Feld

figure **1 B** Figur; **4 B** Zahl

to **figure out** **3 A** herausbekommen,
ausrechnen

to **fill up** **9 B** auffüllen

film star **1 BF** Filmstar

final **2 EP** letzte/r/s

to **finalize** **4 A** festlegen, beschließen

finding **8 BF** Ergebnis, Befund

finger: to keep one's fingers crossed **6 B**
die Daumen drücken

finish **3 B** letzter Schliff, Finish

fire: to put out the ~ **7 B** die Wogen glätten

first: ~ name **1 BF** Vorname; ~ thing **1 A** als erstes, gleich

to fish **3 BF** fischen, angeln

to fit sb in **6 BF** *hier:* jmdn unterbringen

fitted **4 B** *hier:* eingerichtet, angepasst

fix **5 B** fest

flat **1 B** flach

flexibility **5 A** Flexibilität

flexitime **1 A** Gleitzeit

floor: top ~ **5 A** oberste Etage

fluently **6 A** fließend

focus **1 A** Fokus, Mittelpunkt

fog **3 EP** Nebel

foldable **8 BF** klappbar

to follow: as follows **4 A** wie folgt

follower **5 B** Anhänger/in

font **BC** Schrift

footwear **3 A** Schuhwerk

for: ~ a living **1 A** als Beruf, für den Lebensunterhalt; ~ instance **8 A** zum Beispiel; ~ one thing **1 BF** zum einen; to stand ~ **5 EP** stehen für, bedeuten

to forbid **3 B** verbieten, untersagen

to force **4 A** zwingen

forecast **4 A** Prognose, Voraussage

former **2 A** früher, ehemalig

forthcoming **8 A** bevorstehend

to forward **9 A** schicken, nachsenden

to found **1 BF** gründen

foundation **5 B** Stiftung

framework **8 A** Rahmen

franchise **9 EP** Franchise, Lizenz

frequently **3 BF** regelmäßig

fresh **1 B** frisch

from ... onwards **8 B** von ... an

front door **5 B** Vordertür

to fry **9 B** *(in der Pfanne)* braten, frittieren

to fulfill **BC** erfüllen

full **1 BF** vollständig

fun **1 BF** Spaß; to make ~ of sb **9 B** sich über jmdn lustig machen

functionality **5 BF** Funktionalität

funding **10 BF** Gelder, Mittel, Finanzierung

furnished **2 B** eingerichtet, ausgestattet

furniture **1 A** Möbel

furthermore **7 BF** des Weiteren, außerdem

G

to gain **10 EP** gewinnen

gallery **3 BF** Galerie

garlic **9 B** Knoblauch

garment **1 B** Kleidungsstück

gate **3 B** Flugsteig

to generate **1 B** erzeugen

generation **2 B** Generation

gentle **1 EP** vorsichtig

genuine **3 EP** aufrichtig, echt

to get: to ~ across **9 B** vermitteln; to ~ away **1 A** wegkommen, weggehen; to ~ by **1 EP** zurechtkommen; to ~ down to business **3 EP** zum Geschäftlichen übergehen; to ~ in touch **6 B** kontaktieren; to ~ started **1 A** anfangen, loslegen; to ~ sth right **4 BF** etw richtig verstehen; to ~ to do (sth) **1 BF** die Möglichkeit haben, etw zu tun; to ~ to know **9 A** kennenlernen; to ~ to work **1 A** zur Arbeit gehen/kommen; to ~ up **1 A** aufstehen

to give: to ~ sb a rain check **9 EP** auf eine Einladung ein anderes Mal zurückkommen; to ~ sb a wave **10 EP** jmdm zuwinken; to ~ sth a go **5 B** etw ausprobieren; to ~ support **1 A** unterstützen

giveaway **4 BF** Werbeartikel

glad **1 A** glücklich, froh

glance **8 A** Blick; at first ~ **8 A** auf den ersten Blick

to globalize **9 B** globalisieren

glorious **6 BF** fantastisch

glue **1 B** Klebstoff, Leim

to **go**: to ~ **ahead** **1 A** weitermachen; to ~
 Dutch **9 EP** getrennt bezahlen; to ~
 out of business **8 B** Konkurs gehen; to
 ~ **over sth** **4 B** etw durchgehen, durchsehen; to ~ **with sth** **WU** zu etw
 passen; to **give sth a** ~ **5 B** etw ausprobieren

goal **WU** Ziel

to **google** **9 A** googeln

to **graduate** **2 A** einen Abschluss machen

graph: line ~ **4 A** Liniendiagramm

graphic **1 A** Grafik

grateful **3 B** dankbar

greatly **5 A** sehr, stark

grilled **9 B** gegrillt

to **grow** **1 B** wachsen, zunehmen, steigen

growth **10 A** Wachstum

to **guess** **1 B** raten, schätzen, erraten

guideline **3 B** Richtlinie

gummi bear **1 B** Gummibärchen

H

habit **1 B** Gewohnheit, Angewohnheit

hair-care **1 B** Haarpflege

half-trying **5 A** halbherzig

halfway **10 BF** halbwegs, halb, auf
 halbem Weg

half **3 A** Hälfte

hand: ~ **cream** **1 B** Handcreme; ~ **tool**
 3 B Handwerkzeug

handbag **7 B** Handtasche

handling **4 BF** Abwicklung, Bearbeitung;
 ~ **costs** **4 BF** Abwicklungskosten,
 Bearbeitungskosten

hard **8 B** schwer ; to **drive a** ~ **bargain**
 5 A hart verhandeln

harmless **1 EP** harmlos

to **have:** to ~ **left** **7 B** übrig haben; to ~
 second thoughts **5 B** es sich anders
 überlegen, Zweifel haben; to ~ **sth in**
 common with sb **WU** etw mit jmdm
 gemeinsam haben; to ~ **the phone on**
 1 A das Telefon eingeschaltet haben

haves **2 EP** Besitz, die Habe

head **1 A** Leiter/in

to **head:** to ~ **for** **3 B** (in eine Richtung)
 gehen; to ~ **sth up** **1 A** etw leiten

header **3 A** Kopfzeile

headgear **3 B** Kopfbedeckung

headset **7 B** Kopfhörer

health **3 A** Gesundheit

healthy **5 A** gesund

heart **9 B** Herz, Kern; **light-hearted**
 1 EP unbeschwert

heavy **9 B** mächtig, schwer

hectic **2 A** hektisch

to **help out** **3 A** aushelfen

to **hesitate** **BC** zögern

hierarchy **1 EP** Hierarchie

high: ~ **heels** **3 B** Schuhe mit hohen
 Absätzen; to **aim** ~ **10 B** sich hohe
 Ziele setzen; **high-end** **4 A** exklusiv

highland **3 A** Hochland

highlight **9 B** Höhepunkt

to **highlight** **6 A** hervorheben, heraus-
 stellen

to **hike** **3 BF** wandern

hint **BC** Anspielung

to **hire** **1 BF** mieten, leihen

history **2 A** Geschichte, Vorgeschichte

to **hold** **2 B** halten; to ~ **on** **6 BF**
 warten; to ~ **sth up** **9 BF** etw
 verzögern, aufhalten

holding **7 A** Anteil; ~ **company** **7 A**
 Holdinggesellschaft

home: ~ **delivery** **1 BF** Hauszustellung;
 ~ **movie theatre** **5 BF** Heimkino;
 home-made **1 BF** selbstgemacht;
 mobile ~ **9 B** Wohnmobil

homeowner **8 A** Hausbesitzer

hometown **WU** Heimatort, Heimatstadt

honest **2 BF** ehrlich

honesty **9 BF** Ehrlichkeit

honeymoon **7 BF** Hochzeitsreise,
 Flitterwochen

hospital **1 A** Krankenhaus

to **host** **9 B** ausrichten, veranstalten

hot-desking **2 B** Arbeitsplatzwahl nach Verfügbarkeit

house: ~ **style** **9 B** nach Art des Hauses; **in-house** **4 B** intern, innerbetrieblich

however **5 A** wie auch immer

HR = Human Resources **1 A** Personalabteilung

hug **10 EP** Umarmung

humorous **9 B** humorvoll, witzig

humour **6 EP** Humor, Komik; **sense of ~** **9 B** Sinn für Humor

hunt **10 B** Jagd, Suche

to **hurt** **5 B** verletzen, schaden

hybrid **8 A** hybrid, Misch-

hydroelectric **1 B** hydroelektrisch

hydroelectric power station **1 B** Wasserkraftwerk

hygiene **1 B** Hygiene

hypothetical **10 A** hypothetisch

I

identification **10 A** Identifikation

to **ignore** **5 B** ignorieren

illegal **2 EP** illegal

image **4 A** Image, Bild

to **imagine** **1 A** sich vorstellen, annehmen

immediate **1 A** unmittelbar, sofort

impatient **9 B** ungeduldig

to **implement** **10 B** umsetzen, einführen

impolite **1 EP** unhöflich

importance **2 A** Wichtigkeit, Bedeutung

impossible **5 A** unmöglich

impressed **BC** beeindruckt

impression **1 A** Eindruck

impressive **3 BF** beeindruckend

improvement **5 B** Verbesserung

in: ~ **case** **4 B** für den Fall; ~ **due course** **BC** zu gegebener Zeit, zur rechten Zeit; ~ **fact** **1 A** um genau zu sein, eigentlich; ~ **full** **5 BF** vollständig; ~ **particular** **1 EP** vor allem, ganz besonders; ~ **person** **WU** persönlich, selbst; ~ **sight**

6 B in Sicht, ~ **the light of** **8 BF** angesichts; ~ **time** **4 A** rechtzeitig; ~ **total** **5 A** insgesamt; ~ **writing** **5 BF** schriftlich; **back** ~ **2000** **6 A** damals, im Jahr 2000; to **be** ~ **for sth** **4 A** etw zu erwarten haben; to **fit sb** ~ **6 BF** *hier:* jmdn unterbringen; to **hand** ~ **5 GS** einreichen; to **pencil sth** ~ **6 BF** vormerken; to **send sth** ~ **2 EP** etw einschicken; to **throw** ~ **5 A** (gratis) dazugeben

inbox **6 BF** Postfach-Eingang

Inc./Corp. = Incorporated Closed Corporation *(AmE)* **1 B** GmbH

incorporated **1 B** eingetragen; ~ **Closed Corporation, Inc./Corp.** *(AmE)* **1 B** GmbH

incorrect **5 A** nicht korrekt

indeed **3 B** gewiss

indicated **6 BF** angezeigt, markiert

indication **2 B** Anzeichen, Hinweis

indirectness **4 EP** Indirektheit

individual **7 EP** Individuum, Einzelne/r

indoors **7 A** drinnen

industrial **1 B** industriell, Industrie-

to **influence** **5 A** beeinflussen

ingredient **1 B** Zutat

in-house **4 B** intern, innerbetrieblich

to **injure** **5 A** sich verletzen

innovation **1 B** Neuerung, Innovation

to **input** **1 A** eingeben

input terminal **10 BF** Eingabeterminal

to **inspect** **3 B** überprüfen, kontrollieren

to **inspire** **1 BF** inspirieren, anspornen

installation **4 B** Installation, Einrichtung, Einbau

instruction **3 B** Anweisung

insurance **5 A** Versicherung

to **integrate** **2 B** integrieren, sich eingliedern

intention **4 A** Absicht, Vorsatz

interest rate **7 A** Zinsen

internal **2 B** intern

to **interrupt** **4 A** unterbrechen
interval **3 BF** Pause
into: to **be ~ sth** **5 B** sich für etw
interessieren
intriguing **6 A** faszinierend, verblüffend
introductory **3 A** einleitend, einführend
to **invent** **2 BF** erfinden, sich ausdenken
inventory **10 A** Inventar, Warenbestand
to **invite** **2 A** einladen; **to ~ sb out for a
meal** **9 B** jmdn zum Essen einladen
to **invoice sb** **8 B** jmdm eine Rechnung
ausstellen
to **involve** **1 A** einschließen, beinhalten
irritated **9 B** gereizt
issue **4 A** Frage, Thema
to **issue:** to **re-issue** **5 A** neu ausstellen,
neu auflegen
IT = Information Technology **1 A** Informationstechnik, Informatik
it: it's **time to …** **1 A** es ist Zeit für/ um …

J

job: to **be between jobs** **1 A** arbeitslos
sein
joke **9 B** Witz
journal **WU** Zeitung, Zeitschrift
judgement **10 EP** Urteilsvermögen,
Meinung
junior **1 A** Junior-, Assistenz-,
untergeordnet
junior manager **1 A** Nachwuchsführungs-
kraft
just-in-time **10 A** *hier:* bedarfsorientiert

K

to **keep one's fingers crossed** **6 B** die
Daumen drücken
kick-off **7 B** Start, Anfang
kind **WU** Art, Sorte
kindly **4 EP** freundlicherweise
kitchen **1 A** Küche
knife **6 A** Messer
know: to **get to ~** **9 A** kennenlernen

L

lab (*informal:* **laboratory**) **1 A** Labor
landing **3 EP** Landung
landscape **3 BF** Landschaft
last name **1 BF** Nachname
late: at the **latest** **8 B** spätestens
laundry **8 A** Wäsche
law **2 EP** Gesetz, Recht
layer **1 B** Schicht, Ebene
layout **5 A** Anordnung, Aufteilung
lazy **5 B** faul
lead **1 EP** Beispiel, Anhaltspunkt; **~ time**
4 BF Bearbeitungszeit, Lieferzeit
to **lead** **10 EP** führen
leading **6 A** führend
leaf **7 B** Blatt
leaflet **3 B** Informationsblatt, Handzettel
to **lease** **10 B** mieten, leasen
leather **3 A** Leder
to **leave:** to **be left over** **10 BF** übrig
sein; to **have left** **7 B** übrig haben
leave **2 A** Urlaub; **parental ~** **5 B**
Elternzeit, Erziehungsurlaub
legal **1 A** Rechts-, juristisch
to **lend** **1 BF** leihen
less likely **5 A** unwahrscheinlich
level **1 B** Niveau, Grad
to **level off** **4 A** sich einpendeln, gleich
bleiben
lie **1 A** Lüge
lifestyle **3 BF** Lebensstil
light **4 BF** hell; **light-hearted** **1 EP**
unbeschwert
lighting equipment **8 A** Lichtausrüstung
likely: **less ~** **5 A** unwahrscheinlich; **most
~** **4 A** wahrscheinlich
to **limit** **3 BF** begrenzen
limitation **BC** Begrenzung, Beschränkung
limousine **1 BF** Limousine,
Straßenkreuzer
line: **1 A** *hier:* Linie; **assembly ~** **3 B**
Montageband; **~ graph** **4 A** Liniendiagramm

to **link** **10 A** verlinken, verbinden

literature **BC** *hier:* Prospekte

liverwurst **9 B** Leberwurst

loan **7 A** Darlehen

lobby **3 EP** Eingangshalle, Foyer

located **WU** gelegen

Location Sourcing Manager **3 BF**
Leiter/in der Abteilung für Standortsuche

to **lock** **10 A** zuschließen, abschließen

to **log on** **7 B** sich anmelden, einwählen

logical **3 EP** logisch

logo **4 BF** Logo

long-established **1 B** alteingeführt,
alteingesessen

to **look**: to ~ **ahead** **4 A** in die Zukunft
blicken; to ~ **around** **7 A** herumschauen

to **lose** **3 A** verlieren

loss **4 A** Verlust

lost **4 A** verloren

to **love**: would ~ **1 BF** hätte(n) gern,
würde(n) gern

low: to **run** ~ **10 A** sinken, zur Neige
gehen

loyal **1 BF** treu, loyal

Ltd = Limited Company *(BrE)* **1 B** GmbH

M

machinery **3 B** Maschinerie, System

mail order **1 A** Versandhandel

mainland **10 A** Festland

mainly **1 A** hauptsächlich

to **maintain** **5 B** bewahren, aufrecht
erhalten

to **make**: to ~ **fun of sb** **9 B** sich über
jmdn lustig machen

male **3 EP** männlich

to **manage sth** **8 A** etw schaffen, gelingen

manager: **junior** ~ **1 A** Nachwuchs-
führungskraft; **Location Sourcing**
Manager **3 BF** Leiter/in der Abteilung
für Standortsuche; **senior** ~ **1 B**
Abteilungsleiter/in

manually **3 B** von Hand, manuell

manufacturer **1 EP** Hersteller

marital **2 A** ehelich, Ehe-

to **mark** **3 B** markieren

market: ~ **pressure** **4 A** Marktdruck; to
beat sb to the ~ **5 EP** jmdn auf dem
Markt/im Wettbewerb schlagen; to **come**
on the ~ **WU** auf den Markt kommen

mat **5 A** Matte

matching **8 EP** passend

maternity **2 A** Mutterschaft

to **matter** **6 EP** wichtig sein, einen
Unterschied machen

meal: to **invite sb out for a** ~ **9 B** jmdn
zum Essen einladen

meaning **2 A** Bedeutung

meanwhile **5 A** inzwischen

meat **7 B** Fleisch

mechanical **2 A** maschinell, Maschinen-

medium: ~ **rare** **7 B** *Steak:* halb durchgebraten; **medium-sized** **WU** mittelgroß

to **meet** **2 A** *hier:* erfüllen; to ~ **a**
standard **1 B** eine Norm erfüllen, einem
Standard entsprechen; to ~ **up with sb**
1 A sich mit jmdm treffen

membership **5 A** Mitgliedschaft

memo **4 B** Kurzmitteilung, Aktennotiz

memorable **1 BF** unvergesslich,
einprägsam

memory stick **4 BF** USB-Stick

menu **4 BF** Menü

merchandise **3 BF** Ware(n)

merger **1 A** Fusion, Zusammenschluss

microchip **9 BF** Mikrochip

microscope **1 A** Mikroskop

mind **2 B** Verstand, Gedanken; to **change**
your ~ **5 BF** es sich anders überlegen

minimum **3 B** Mindest-

mint **3 BF** Minze, Pfefferminze

minty **3 BF** Pfefferminz-

mobile home **9 B** Wohnmobil

mobility **9 B** Mobilität, Beweglichkeit

model 8 BF Modell
morale 4 B *hier:* Stimmung
moreover 8 A zudem, ferner
mortgage 7 A Hypothek
most likely 4 A wahrscheinlich
to **motivate** 5 A motivieren
to **move: to ~ around** 1 A umherbewegen, transportieren
mug 4 BF Tasse
multinational 1 EP multinational
museum 1 BF Museum
mushroom 9 B Pilz
mutual 7 A beiderseitig, gemeinsam

N

name: brand ~ 1 B Markenname; **first ~**
1 BF Vorname; **last ~** 1 BF Nachname
nappy 1 B Windel
native WU gebürtig, einheimisch; **~**
speaker WU Muttersprachler/in; **non-**
native speaker WU Nichtmutter-
sprachler/in
natural 1 B natürlich, Natur-
neck of the woods *(coll.)* 8 B Gegend
need 2 A Bedürfnis
negotiator 5 A Händler/in
net 4 A netto, Netto-
nevertheless 8 A trotzdem
nonetheless 8 A trotzdem, nichtsdesto-
weniger
non: non-native speaker WU Nicht-
muttersprachler/in; **non-smoking** 7 B
Nichtraucher-
noodle 3 BF Nudel
noon 1 EP Mittag
norm 2 EP Norm, Regel
not: ~ at all 1 A überhaupt nicht; **~ only**
... but also ... 8 A nicht nur ..., sondern
auch ...
notebook 2 EP Notizbuch
notepaper 4 BF Briefpapier
to **notice** 6 B bemerken
nowadays 2 EP heutzutage

number-cruncher 1 BF jmd, der gut mit
Zahlen umgehen kann

O

to **obtain** BC erhalten
obviously 1 B natürlich, selbstverständlich
off: kick-off 7 B Start, Anfang; to **level**
~ 4 A sich einpendeln, gleich bleiben
Officer: CEO = Chief Executive ~ 1 A
Geschäftsführer/in, Vorstandschef/in;
CFO = Chief Financial ~ 1 A Finanz-
chef/in, Leiter/in der Finanzabteilung;
CIO = Chief Information ~ 1 A
Leiter/in der Abteilung Informations-
technologie; **COO = Chief Operating**
~ 1 A Betriebsleiter/in; **CRO = Chief**
Risk ~ 1 A Risikomanager/in; **CTO =**
Chief Technology ~ 1 A Technische
Direktorin / Technischer Direktor
official 2 A offiziell
offsite 7 B extern
oil 1 A Öl
old-fashioned 1 BF altmodisch
on: ~ a regular basis 1 B regelmäßig;
~ average 5 B im Durchschnitt; **~ file**
4 BF in den Akten; **~ site** 9 A vor Ort;
~ standby 4 B in Bereitschaft; **~ the**
other hand 8 A andererseits; **~ the**
premises 3 B im Hause; to **have the**
phone ~ 1 A das Telefon eingeschaltet
haben; to **hold ~** 6 BF warten; to **log**
~ 7 B sich anmelden, einwählen
one: one-liner 6 EP Einzeiler; **one-time**
3 A einmalig
ongoing 4 B fortlaufend, andauernd
only 9 A erst
onto 6 EP auf
Open Corporation *(AmE)* 1 B AG
opening 1 A *hier:* freie Stelle
operator 4 B Bediener/in, Anwender/in
opportunity 2 A Gelegenheit
optimization 4 B Optimierung
to **optimize** 2 B optimieren

option **5 B** Möglichkeit, Option, Wahl

or: either ... or ... **1 A** entweder ... oder ...

order: mail ~ **1 A** Versandhandel

ordinary **3 EP** gewöhnlich, alltäglich

organization **1 B** Organisation, Unternehmen, Einteilung

organizer **8 A** Organisator/in, Veranstalter/in

origin **9 B** Ursprung, Herkunft

originally **WU** ursprünglich

otherwise **1 BF** sonst, ansonsten

out: ~ of balance **5 B** aus dem Gleich- gewicht; to act ~ **7 A** durchspielen; to bring ~ **4 A** herausbringen; to burn ~ **5 B** ausbrennen, sich kaputt machen; to cross ~ **6 A** streichen; to eat ~ **4 A** essen gehen; to figure ~ **3 A** heraus- bekommen, ausrechnen; to go ~ of business **8 B** Konkurs gehen; to help ~ **3 A** aushelfen; to put ~ the fire **7 B** die Wogen glätten; to reach ~ **1 BF** *hier:* seine Fühler ausstrecken; to read ~ **1 A** vorlesen; to sort ~ **7 B** in Ordnung bringen, aufräumen; to stand ~ **1 BF** auffallen, hervorstechen

outlet **8 A** Laden, Geschäftsstelle

to outline **7 BF** skizzieren, umreißen

outskirts **2 A** Stadtrand, Außenbezirke

oven **9 B** Ofen

over: all ~ **WU** überall; to be left ~ **10 BF** übrig sein; to go ~ sth **4 B** etw durchgehen, durchsehen

overall **4 A** allgemein, gesamt, Gesamt-

to overcook **7 B** verkochen

to overdo **6 EP** übertreiben

to overestimate **10 B** überschätzen

overseas **9 A** Auslands-, ausländisch

overview **4 A** Überblick

to own **5 B** besitzen

P

to package **8 A** verpacken; pre-packaged **8 A** abgepackt

page: three-page **6 A** dreiseitig

painting **2 EP** Malerei, Malen

parent company **1 B** Muttergesellschaft

parental **5 B** elterlich; ~ leave **5 B** Elternzeit, Erziehungsurlaub

particular **1 EP** bestimmt, speziell, besondere/r/s

particularly **6 BF** besonders

partnership **9 B** Zusammenarbeit, Partnerschaft

party **5 A** Partei

past **2 A** Vergangenheit

past **4 A** letzte/r/s *(zeitlich)*

pastry **1 A** Gebäck(stück)

paternity **2 A** Vaterschaft

pattern **3 B** Muster, Vorlage

pause **6 EP** Pause

to pay: to ~ back **7 A** zurückzahlen

payroll **1 A** Gehaltsrechnung

pea **9 B** Erbse

to peak **4 A** den Höhepunkt/die Spitze erreichen

peanuts **7 B** Erdnüsse

to pencil sth in **6 BF** vormerken

percentage **3 A** Prozentsatz, Anteil

perfume **9 B** Parfum

peripheral **10 A** nebensächlich, Rand-

permalink **8 EP** Permalink

personal **2 EP** persönlich, privat

personalization **10 A** Personalisierung

personalized **10 A** personalisiert, individuell gestaltet

personally **1 A** persönlich

to persuade **2 B** überreden, überzeugen

pharmaceutical **1 EP** pharmazeutisch

phase **4 B** Phase

phased **5 B** gestuft; ~ retirement **5 B** Altersteilzeit

phone: to have the ~ on **1 A** das Telefon eingeschaltet haben

physical **7 B** körperlich, physisch

to pick **3 BF** aussuchen, auswählen; to ~ up **6 B** abholen

pick-up **3 A** Abholung

picnic **10 B** Picknick

pioneering **6 A** bahnbrechend

pitch **6 B** Wurf, *hier:* Präsentation, Verkaufsgespräch

to pitch **10 A** *hier:* anbieten

plant **1 B** Fabrik, Werk, Maschinen

platform **7 BF** Plattform

platinum **9 BF** Platin

playful **8 BF** verspielt

plc = Public Limited Company *(BrE)* **1 B** AG

pleasant **2 B** angenehm

plenty of **9 B** reichlich

point: ~ of view **9 BF** Standpunkt, Perspektive; **to the ~** **8 EP** kurz, präzise; **walk-away ~** **5 A** Schmerzgrenze

polite **4 EP** höflich

politeness **4 EP** Höflichkeit

pollution **8 A** Verschmutzung

poor **1 BF** arm, armselig

popularity **2 B** Popularität, Beliebtheit

pork **9 B** Schweinefleisch

portion **7 B** Portion

post **6 A** Posten

to post **6 A** *(online)* posten

postcard **4 EP** Postkarte

potential **2 EP** potentiell

power **1 B** *hier:* Strom, Energie; **hydroelectric ~ station** **1 B** Wasserkraftwerk

to predict **4 A** vorher-/voraussagen, prophezeien

preference **3 BF** Vorliebe

premier **4 A** Spitzen-, Top-, führend

premise **3 B** Prämisse, Voraussetzung

premium **1 B** erstklassig, Spitzen-

pre-packaged **8 A** abgepackt

preparation **5 A** Vorbereitung

presence **9 A** Präsenz, Anwesenheit

to present **7 A** präsentieren

presenter **7 BF** Moderator/in, Referent/in

president **9 A** Präsident/in, Vorsitzende/r

to press **4 BF** drücken

pressure **4 A** Druck

pretty **2 BF** ziemlich

price: price-conscious **8 A** preisbewusst; **asking ~** **5 A** geforderter Preis; **to be priced** **8 A** kosten

printout **7 B** Ausdruck

probably **1 A** wahrscheinlich

procedure **2 EP** Vorgehen, Verfahren

process **3 A** Prozess

processing **6 A** Herstellung, Bearbeitung

producer **2 A** Hersteller

production: ~ line **1 A** Produktionsanlage, Fertigungslinie; **~ site** **3 A** Fertigungsstätte

productivity **10 BF** Produktivität, Leistung

professional **2 A** beruflich

professionals **1 BF** Fachleute

to profile **1 A** ein Profil erstellen

progress **6 B** Fortschritt

to project **8 B** planen

projection **4 B** Voraussage, Prognose

to promise **2 BF** versprechen

to promote sth **8 A** für etw Werbung machen

prompt **2 A** Stichwort

to pronounce **8 B** aussprechen

properly **6 EP** richtig, anständig

property **7 A** Eigentum, Immobilie

proposal **5 A** Vorschlag

to propose **6 BF** vorschlagen

proposition **10 A** Vorschlag, Angebot

pros and cons **2 B** Pro und Contra

to protect **9 BF** schützen

protective **3 B** Schutz-, schützend

prototype **6 B** Prototyp

proud(ly) **BC** stolz

provider **8 A** Anbieter/in

provisional **6 BF** provisorisch, vorläufig

to publish **2 B** veröffentlichen

punctuation **BC** Zeichensetzung, Interpunktion

purchasing **1 A** Einkauf

purely **1 A** rein

purpose **7 BF** Zweck, Absicht

to **push**: to ~ **up** **4 A** in die Höhe treiben

to **put**: to ~ **out the fire** **7 B** die Wogen glätten

pyramid **1 B** Pyramide

Q

query **4 BF** Frage

to **query** **8 B** fragen

R

R&D = Research and Development **1 A** Forschung und Entwicklung

racquet **5 BF** Schläger

rain: to **give a ~ check** **9 EP** auf eine Einladung ein anderes Mal zurückkommen

rapid **2 A** schnell

rapport **7 BF** Verhältnis

rare **7 B** *Steak:* blutig; **medium ~** **7 B** halb durchgebraten

rate: interest ~ **7 A** Zinsen

rather **1 BF** ziemlich; **4 EP** eher, lieber

to **reach**: to ~ **out** **1 BF** *hier:* seine Fühler ausstrecken

to **react** **1 EP** reagieren

to **read**: to ~ **back** **1 BF** nochmal vorlesen; to ~ **out** **1 A** vorlesen

reader **1 A** Leser/in

to **realize** **8 B** bemerken, realisieren

rearrange **1 EP** umstellen, ändern

reasonable **8 A** vernünftig

rebate **5 BF** Rabatt, Preisnachlass

recent **3 B** jüngst, aktuell

recognition **2 B** Anerkennung

recommendation **3 B** Empfehlung

to **record** **1 A** aufnehmen

record: drug ~ **1 EP** Medikamenten-register/ -verzeichnis

recruitment agency **BC** Arbeits-vermittlung

recyclable **8 A** wiederverwendbar

to **recycle** **8 A** wiederverwerten

to **refer to** **7 BF** sich beziehen auf

to **reformulate** **7 BF** umformulieren

refreshment **1 A** Erfrischung, Imbiss

to **refund** **5 BF** rückerstatten, zurückzahlen

to **refuse** **3 BF** ablehnen

region **1 B** Region, Gebiet, Gegend

regulation **3 A** Vorschrift, Bestimmung

to **reimburse** **BC** entschädigen

reimbursement **1 A** Erstattung, Rück-zahlung

to **re-issue** **5 A** neu ausstellen, neu auflegen

to **reject** **5 A** ablehnen, zurückweisen

to **relate** **10 B** in Zusammenhang bringen

related **1 A** zusammenhängend

relationship-building **8 EP** beziehungs-stärkend

relatively **5 BF** relativ

to **release** **2 B** veröffentlichen, herausbringen

relevant **2 A** relevant, einschlägig

relief **8 EP** Erleichterung

relocation **9 A** Standortwechsel, Versetzung

remark **3 A** Bemerkung

remote **7 BF** weit entfernt

to **remove** **3 B** (weg-)transportieren; **5 B** wegnehmen, entfernen

renewable **8 A** erneuerbar

renovation **7 BF** Renovierung

rental **1 BF** Verleih

to **rephrase** **8 A** umformulieren, anders ausdrücken

to **replace** **8 B** ersetzen, austauschen

to **report to sb** **1 A** jmdm unterstellt sein

representative **8 B** Vertreter/in

to **request sth** **2 EP** um etw bitten

to **reschedule** **6 B** verlegen

resource: ~ centre **9 EP** Informations-zentrum; **HR = Human Resources** **1 A** Personalabteilung rest **1 B** Rest

résumé *(AmE)* **2 A** Lebenslauf

retail **1 A** Einzelhandel

retirement **5 B** Ruhestand

to return **2 BF** zurückkommen; to ~ a
call **1 BF** zurückrufen

reusable **8 A** wiederverwendbar

revenue **2 B** Einkünfte, Einnahmen

to revolutionize **9 A** revolutionieren,
grundlegend verändern

rewarding **6 A** lohnend

to rewrite **2 EP** umschreiben

rhetorical **7 BF** rhetorisch

right: to get sth ~ **4 BF** etw richtig
verstehen

to ring **2 EP** klingeln

to roast **9 B** *(im Ofen)* braten, rösten,
schmoren

to role-play **9 BF** ein Rollenspiel machen

room **5 A** *hier:* Raum, Platz

roomy **8 A** geräumig

root **9 A** Wurzel, Stamm

rotating **1 A** rotierend

round: all-round **8 BF** vielseitig,
Allround-; to buy a ~ **9 EP** eine Runde
ausgeben

rumour **9 B** Gerücht

to run: to ~ a company **WU** ein Geschäft
führen, betreiben; to ~ low **10 A**
sinken, zur Neige gehen

S

sabbatical **3 A** Forschungsurlaub, Sabbat-
jahr

safety: ~ engineer **1 A** Sicherheits-
ingenieur/in, Sicherheitstechniker/in

sales **1 A** Verkauf

salt sticks **7 B** Salzstangen

salted **7 B** gesalzen

salty **9 B** salzig

sandal **1 B** Sandale

satisfaction **5 B** Zufriedenheit,
Befriedigung

satisfactory **BC** ausreichend, befriedigend

satisfied **4 BF** zufrieden

sauce **9 B** Soße

sausage **9 B** Wurst

to save **2 EP** sparen

savings **10 BF** Ersparnisse

to say: say … **2 BF** *hier:* zum Beispiel …;
as they ~ **5 A** wie man sagt

to scan **10 A** scannen

schedule: to be behind ~ **2 A** im Verzug
sein; to stay on ~ **4 B** im Zeitplan
bleiben

to schedule **7 B** ansetzen, planen

scheme **5 B** Schema

seasonal **10 A** Saison-, jahreszeitlich

second **1 BF** Sekunde

second: to have ~ thoughts **5 B** es sich
anders überlegen, Zweifel haben

secondary **10 A** zweitrangig, sekundär

security **2 A** Sicherheit

segment **4 A** Segment, Teil

to select **4 B** auswählen

selection **5 BF** Auswahl

self **1 BF** selbst

to send: to ~ sth in **2 EP** etw einschicken;
to ~ up **7 B** hochschicken

senior **1 A** leitend; ~ manager **1 B**
Abteilungsleiter/in

sense: ~ of humour **9 B** Sinn für Humor

sensitive **7 B** heikel

sequence **3 EP** Reihenfolge

series **7 A** Serie, Reihe

to serve **1 BF** bedienen; **9 B** servieren

server **9 B** Kellner

set **7 B** Set, Satz, Paar, Garnitur

to set **1 B** setzen, stellen, legen; to ~ up
7 B arrangieren, einrichten; to be ~ in
stone **4 A** unverrückbar sein

several **1 A** mehrere, einige

to sew **3 B** nähen

sex **2 A** Geschlecht

shame **6 B** Schande, Scham

shape **3 B** Form

shift **4 B** Schicht

shin **6 EP** Schienbein

shocking **8 BF** schockierend; ~ **pink**
8 BF grelles Pink

shoemaker **3 A** Schuhmacher/in

shoemaking **3 B** Schuhmacherei,
-fabrikation

shop: to **talk** ~ **3 EP** über die Arbeit
reden, fachsimpeln

to **shorten 5 B** verkürzen, kürzen

short-term **10 A** kurzfristig

to **shrug 6 EP** mit den Achseln zucken

side dish **9 B** Beilage

sign **4 A** Zeichen

significant **8 EP** bedeutend, erheblich

similar **1 BF** ähnlich

simple **3 A** einfach

simultaneous **7 BF** gleichzeitig, simultan

since: **ever** ~ **9 B** seitdem

sincere **10 EP** aufrichtig, ehrlich

single **5 BF** einfach

to **sit down 1 A** sich hinsetzen

sitemap **1 B** Seitenübersicht, Strukturkarte

sized: **medium-sized WU** mittelgroß

skiing **2 A** Skifahren

skilled **3 B** Fach-, geschickt, ausgebildet

skin **8 A** Haut

slang **8 B** Slang, Jargon

slowly **1 EP** langsam

smart **3 A** schick, fein

to **smoke 3 B** rauchen

smooth **9 A** reibungslos, problemlos

smoothly **3 A** reibungslos, problemlos

snack **9 B** Snack

so: ~ **far 7 A** bis jetzt, bisher; ~ **to speak**
3 B sozusagen; **so-called 7 B** soge-
nannte/r/s

soap **1 B** Seife

social **1 A** privat, sozial, gesellschaftlich

to **soften 4 EP** abschwächen

solar panel **8 A** Sonnenkollektor

sole **3 B** Sohle

solid **2 B** fest

to **solve 7 B** lösen

someplace **6 B** irgendwohin

to **sort:** to ~ **out 7 B** in Ordnung bringen,
aufräumen

source: **Location Sourcing Manager**
3 BF Leiter/in der Abteilung für Standortsuche

space **1 B** Raum

spare **4 EP** Ersatz-

to **spare 10 B** entbehren

spare time **10 B** Freizeit

sparkling **7 B** schäumend; ~ **water 7 B**
kohlensäurehaltiges Mineralwasser

speaker: **native** ~ **WU** Muttersprach-
ler/in; **non-native** ~ **WU** Nicht-
muttersprachler/in

special: **today's** ~ **7 EP** Tagesgericht

speciality **3 BF** Spezialität

to **specialize (in sth) 1 B** sich (auf etw)
spezialisieren

specially **5 A** speziell

specialty **9 A** Spezialität

specific **1 BF** präzise, spezifisch

to **specify 1 EP** angeben

speculation **8 BF** Spekulation, Vermutung

speed **8 BF** *hier:* Gang; to **bring sb up to**
~ **4 A** jmdn auf den neuesten Stand
bringen **computing** ~ **10 BF** Rechner-
geschwindigkeit

to **speed up 10 B** beschleunigen

speedy **1 BF** schnell

to **spend:** to ~ **time on sth 1 A** Zeit
verbringen mit etw

spicy **3 BF** würzig, pikant

spontaneous **7 BF** spontan

to **spot 1 A** entdecken

spouse **6 A** Ehepartner/in

to **spy 9 B** spionieren

stain **8 A** Fleck

to **stand:** to ~ **for 5 EP** stehen für, bedeuten; to ~ **out 1 BF** auffallen,
hervorstechen; **stand-alone 8 B** alleinstehend, freistehend

standard: to meet a ~ **1 B** eine Norm erfüllen, einem Standard entsprechen

standby **4 B** Reserve

stand-up **6 A** Steh-

star: film ~ **1 BF** Filmstar

start: to ~ up **1 BF** gründen; to get started **1 A** anfangen, loslegen

to state **4 EP** erklären, darstellen

station **1 B** Station; hydroelectric power ~ **1 B** Wasserkraftwerk

stationary **3 B** gleichbleibend

status **2 A** Status, Stand

to stay: to ~ on schedule **4 B** im Zeitplan bleiben

steady **1 A** fest, zuverlässig

steam **9 BF** Dampf; to let off ~ (coll.) **9 BF** Dampf ablassen

steel **8 A** Stahl

step **8 BF** hier: Einstieg

stereo: car ~ **10 B** Autoradio

stick: **4 BF** Stab, Stock; memory ~ **4 BF** USB-Stick; salt sticks **7 B** Salzstangen

still: ~ water **7 B** Mineralwasser ohne Kohlensäure

to stock sth **WU** etw lagern, führen

stone: to be set in ~ **4 A** unverrückbar sein

to stop: to ~ by **7 A** vorbeikommen

storage **10 A** Lagerung, Computer: Speicherung

straightforward **1 B** einfach

strength **10 B** Stärke, Kraft

to strengthen **10 EP** stärken, verstärken

to stress **2 A** betonen

stressed **5 B** gestresst

strictly **3 B** streng

to strike **8 EP** aufschlagen, auftreffen; to ~ the right tone **8 EP** den richtigen Ton treffen

stroll **3 B** Spaziergang, Bummel

stuck **9 A** festgeklebt, festgeklemmt; to be stucked **9 A** stecken bleiben, festsitzen

sturdy **3 A** robust, stabil

style: block ~ **BC** Blocksatz; house ~ **9 B** nach Art des Hauses

sub **3 A** Unter-

to subscribe **9 B** abonnieren, beziehen

subscriber **9 A** Abonnent/in, Empfänger/in

subsidiary **WU** Tochtergesellschaft

substantial **8 A** beträchtlich, erheblich

subtitle **BC** Untertitel

to succeed **8 B** Erfolg haben, erfolgreich sein

such as **8 A** wie beispielsweise

sufficient **10 EP** genügend

sugar **1 EP** Zucker

to suit **6 BF** passen

suitcase **3 A** Koffer

to sum: to ~ up **8 A** resümieren, zusammenfassen

to summarize **1 A** zusammenfassen

sunrise **9 BF** Sonnenaufgang

superficial **3 EP** oberflächlich

superior **8 A** ausgezeichnet, hervorragend

to supervise **1 A** betreuen, leiten, überwachen

supervisor **1 A** Leiter/in

support **1 A** Unterstützung; to give ~ **1 A** unterstützen

to suppose **6 BF** annehmen, glauben

to surf **6 BF** surfen

surprisingly **1 B** überraschenderweise

survey **2 B** Überblick

sustainability **1 B** Nachhaltigkeit, Umweltschutz

sustainable **8 A** nachhaltig, umweltgerecht

sweet **9 B** Süßigkeit, Nachspeise

sweet **9 B** süß

sweetness **9 B** Süße

to switch **2 A** tauschen, wechseln

switch **3 B** Schalter

syllable **2 A** Silbe

to sympathize **9 BF** Verständnis haben

synthetic **3 B** synthetisch

T

tab **9 EP** Rechnung
table **7 B** *hier:* Tabelle
tablet **8 B** *hier:* Tablette
tag **5 A** Schild, Etikett
to take: to ~ a break **1 A** eine Pause
  machen; to ~ into account **8 BF**
  berücksichtigen; to ~ part in sth **WU**
  an etw teilnehmen; to ~ pictures **10 A**
  Fotos machen; to ~ the blame **9 BF** die
  Schuld auf sich nehmen; to ~ things
  slowly **9 B** Dinge langsam angehen; to
  ~ turns **WU** sich abwechseln
takeover **9 A** Übernahme
to talk: to ~ shop **3 EP** über die Arbeit
  reden, fachsimpeln
to target **1 B** zielen auf
taste **8 BF** Geschmack
to taste **3 B** schmecken
to teach **1 B** lehren
technique **7 BF** Technik, Methode
technologically **8 A** technologisch
Technology: IT = Information ~ **1 A**
  Informationstechnik, Informatik
teleconference **WU** Konferenzschaltung,
  Telekonferenz
temporary **2 A** befristet, vorübergehend
tense **3 A** Zeit
term **4 BF** Bedingung; terms of
  payment **4 BF** Zahlungsbedingungen;
  short-term **10 A** kurzfristig
terminal: input ~ **10 BF** Eingabeterminal
terrain **3 A** Gelände, Terrain
testing **4 B** Testen, Prüfen
to text **5 B** eine SMS schreiben
the day before yesterday **7 EP**
  vorgestern
to the point **8 EP** sachdienlich
theme **BC** Thema
then **2 A** damals
therefore **8 A** deshalb

these days **1 BF** heutzutage
thirsty **7 B** durstig
thoroughly **3 B** gründlich
though **4 EP** trotzdem, aber, dennoch
thought: to have second thoughts **5 B**
  es sich anders überlegen, Zweifel haben
threat **10 B** Gefahr
three-page **6 A** dreiseitig
thrilled **3 BF** begeistert, sehr froh
throughout **1 B** überall
to throw in **5 A** (gratis) dazugeben
thus **6 A** so, demzufolge
tie **3 EP** Krawatte
to tie **9 EP** binden, anbinden; to be tied
  up **9 EP** dienstlich verhindert sein
tier **10 A** Ebene, Rang, Stufe; ~ one
  supplier **10 A** Lieferant der ersten
  Ebene
time: it's time to **1 A** es ist Zeit für/um
  ...; just-in-time **10 A** bedarfsorientiert;
  lead ~ **4 BF** Bearbeitungszeit, Lieferzeit;
  spare ~ **10 B** Freizeit; to spend ~ on
  sth **1 A** Zeit verbringen mit etw
tissue **8 A** Papiertaschentuch
today's special **7 EP** Tagesgericht
tool **3 B** Werkzeug; hand ~ **3 B** Handwerkzeug
to top **9 B** *hier:* überziehen, garnieren
top **1 B** Spitze
top **5 A** oberste/r/s; ~ floor **5 A** oberste
  Etage
to touch **3 B** berühren; to ~ base **6**
  B sich bei jmdm melden
touch **7 A** Note, Touch; to get in ~ **6 B**
  jmdn kontaktieren; ~ screen **10**
  A Touchscreen, Berührungsbildschirm
tough **5 A** zäh, ausdauernd, hart
toxic **8 A** giftig
track **6 A** Kurs, Pfad, Spur; to be back
  on ~ **7 B** wieder auf dem richtigen Weg
  sein; ~ record **6 A** Erfolgsgeschichte,
  Leistung
tractor **1 BF** Traktor

trade **WU** Fach, Branche, Gewerbe, Handel; ~ **journal WU** Fachzeitschrift, Handelsblatt; ~ **directory BC** Branchenadressbuch

traffic **6 EP** Verkehr

trained **5 A** trainiert, geschult

trainee **1 A** Auszubildende/r, Trainee

training **1 A** Ausbildung, Einarbeitung, Schulung; ~ **programme 9 A** Mitarbeitertraining, Schulungsprogramm

trait **7 EP** Merkmal

transfer **9 A** Versetzung, Transfer, Wechsel

transition **4 B** Übergang

translation **3 A** Übersetzung

translator **10 B** Übersetzer/in

to travel **5 A** *hier:* hinfahren

travel expenses **7 B** Reisekosten

treasure **10 B** Schatz

treat **1 BF** Vergnügen, Genuss, etwas Besonderes

to treat sb to sth **9 EP** jmdn zu etw einladen

tree **8 A** Baum

trek **3 BF** Marsch, Treck

trial **4 B** Test, Probe

tricky **1 EP** schwierig, verzwickt

trouble **7 B** Schwierigkeiten, Ärger, Probleme

true to **9 A** getreu

to trust **10 B** vertrauen

trusted **1 B** zuverlässig, vertraut

to try: half-trying **5 A** halbherzig

to turn: to ~ **down 9 EP** ablehnen; to ~ **off 7 B** ausschalten

turnover **4 A** Umsatz

tyre **9 EP** Reifen

U

unacceptable **2 BF** nicht akzeptabel

uncomfortable **3 EP** unangenehm, peinlich

to undergo **2 B** sich unterziehen

understaffed **2 B** unterbesetzt

understatement **1 EP** Untertreibung, Understatement

to undertake **8 BF** vornehmen, durchführen

unexpected **6 BF** unerwartet

unexpectedly **4 A** unerwartet

unfamiliar **6 A** unbekannt

unfortunately **4 A** unglücklicherweise

union **4 A** Vereinigung, Verband

unique **1 BF** einzigartig, einmalig

unless **10 B** wenn nicht, es sei denn

unlike **4 A** anders als

to unload **3 B** abladen, entladen

to unpack **3 B** auspacken

unrealistic **4 B** unrealistisch

unreasonable **10 B** unvernünftig

unsuccessful **2 EP** erfolglos

to upgrade **2 EP** *hier:* aufrüsten

to upload **7 B** hochladen

up: back-up **4 B** Reserve, Ersatz; to bring sb ~ to date **10 BF** jmdn auf den neuesten Stand bringen; to bring sb ~ to speed **4 A** jmdn auf den neuesten Stand bringen; to come ~ **6 BF** dazwischenkommen; to fill ~ **9 B** auffüllen; to get ~ **1 A** aufstehen; to head sth ~ **1 A** leiten; to hold sth ~ **9 BF** etw verzögern, aufhalten; to meet ~ with sb **1 A** sich mit jmdm treffen; to push ~ **4 A** in die Höhe treiben; to send ~ **7 B** hochschicken; to speed ~ **10 B** beschleunigen; stand-up **6 A** Steh-; to sum ~ **8 A** resümieren, zusammenfassen; to use sth ~ **5 A** etw aufbrauchen; to wrap ~ **3 B** einpacken

upper **3 B** obere/r/s

urgently **3 A** dringend

use **3 A** Gebrauch, Einsatz

to use: to ~ sth up **5 A** etw aufbrauchen

used **5 A** gebraucht; ~ to do sth **2 A** früher etw getan haben

useless **5 B** nutzlos

user **10 A** Nutzer/in

usual 2 EP üblich, normal

utility 1 B Nutzen, *hier:* Versorgungs-
betrieb; **~ company** 1 B Elektrizitäts-
werk, Energieversorger

V

valued BC geschätzt, gewürdigt

vanilla 1 B Vanille

variation 10 A Variante, Variation

various 1 B verschiedene

to vary BC variieren, sich ändern

veal 9 B Kalbfleisch

vegetable 9 EP Gemüse

vegetarian 3 BF vegetarisch

vehicle 1 BF Fahrzeug

vending WU Verkauf; **~ machine** WU
(Verkaufs-)Automat

venue BC Veranstaltungsort

via 7 B über, per, via

vibrant 1 B dynamisch

vice versa 5 A umgekehrt

view: point of ~ 9 BF Standpunkt,
Perspektive

village 1 BF Dorf

vintage 1 BF alt, altmodisch, klassisch;
~ car 1 BF Oldtimer

virtual 7 B virtuell

vision 1 B Vision

voicemail 8 B Mailbox

volunteer 7 BF Freiwillige/r

W

wages 1 EP Lohn

to wake up 7 B aufwachen

wake up call 7 B Weckruf

walk-away point 5 A Schmerzgrenze

walking lunch 5 B Spaziergang in der
Mittagspause

want 2 EP Wunsch, Bedürfnis

water: sparkling ~ 7 B kohlensäurehaltiges Mineralwasser; **still ~** 7 B
Mineralwasser ohne Kohlensäure

wave: to give sb a ~ 10 EP jmdm
zuwinken

way: to come your ~ 2 B einem über den
Weg laufen

weakness 10 B Schwäche

to wear 3 A *Kleidung:* tragen

webcam 7 B Webcam, Internetkamera

webinar 6 A interaktives Onlineseminar

weights 5 A Gewichte; **~ machine** 5 A
Trainingsgerät mit Gewichten

welcome package 3 B Willkommens-
Paket

well: well-being 5 A Wohlbefinden;
well-off 8 A wohlhabend

what kind of WU was für, welche

whatever 4 A was auch immer

wheat 9 B Weizen

wheel 3 BF Rad

whereabouts 3 A *hier:* wo

whether 8 EP ob

while 2 B während

to whip 9 B schlagen; **whipped cream**
9 B Schlagsahne

white 4 BF weiß; **~ lie** 9 BF Notlüge

whole 4 B ganz

wholesale 2 B Großhandels-

wholesaler 8 A Großhändler/in

whose 6 A deren/dessen

widescreen TV 5 BF Großbildfernseher

willingness 9 BF Bereitschaft

winery WU Weingut

winner 5 A Gewinner/in

wireless 2 B kabellos

with: to connect ~ sb 1 EP mit jmdm in
Verbindung treten; **to go ~ sth** WU zu
etw passen; **to have sth in common ~
sb** WU etw mit jmdm gemeinsam haben

to wonder 1 B sich fragen

work: to get to ~ 1 A zur Arbeit gehen/
kommen; **~ habits** 1 B Arbeitsein-
stellung; **works council** 2 B Betriebsrat

workday 1 A Arbeitstag

workforce 1 B Belegschaft, Arbeitskräfte

workload **5 B** Arbeitspensum
worried **9 A** besorgt, beunruhigt
worthwhile **3 EP** lohnend
would: ~ love **1 BF** hätte(n) gern,
würde(n) gern
to wrap: to ~ up **3 B** einpacken

X
X-ray **4 BF** Röntgenstrahl

Y
Yankee **4 BF** Nordstaatler
yearly **2 EP** jährlich
yesterday: the day before ~ **7 EP** vorgestern
yogurt **WU** Joghurt

Places, countries, nationalities

Ankara	['æŋkərə] 🔊 2.2		Mediterranean	[ˌmedɪtə'reɪnɪən] 68
Atlanta	[ət'læntə] 108		Melbourne	['melbɔːn] 9
Austrian	['ɒstrɪən] 153		Milan	[mɪ'læn] 9
Bangalore	[ˌbæŋgə'lɔː] 19		Morocco	[mə'rɒkəʊ] 78
Berne	[bɜːn] 🔊 1.21		Northern Europe	[ˌnɔːðən 'jʊərəp] 8
Bondi Beach	[ˌbɒndaɪ 'biːtʃ] 🔊 2.9		Norwegian	[nɔː'wiːdʒn] 🔊 1.5
Brighton	['braɪtən] 162		Nuremberg	['njʊərəmbɜːg] 31
British Isles	[ˌbrɪtɪʃ 'aɪlz] 68		Ohio	[əʊ'haɪəʊ] 8
Cape Town	['keɪp taʊn] 8		Oslo	['ɒzləʊ] 🔊 1.5
Chile	['tʃɪli] 🔊 2.2		Paris	['pærɪs] 19
Cleveland	['kliːvlənd] 8		Portugal	['pɔːtʃʊgl] 63
Cologne	[kə'ləʊn] 8		Quebec	[kwɪ'bek] 53
Czech Republic	[ˌtʃek ri'pʌblɪk] 🔊 1.21		Scandinavia	[ˌskændɪ'neɪvɪə] 68
Dublin	['dʌblɪn] 🔊 1.38		Shanghai	[ˌʃæŋ'haɪ] 75
Dutch	[dʌtʃ] 52		Shannon	['ʃænən] 118
England	['ɪŋglənd] 🔊 1.21		Sheffield	['ʃefiːld] 🔊 1.4
Georgia	['dʒɔːdʒə] 108		Spain	[speɪn] 9
Hollywood	['hɒliwʊd] 🔊 1.9		Swiss	[swɪs] 🔊 1.24
Ireland	['aɪələnd] 🔊 1.38		Switzerland	['swɪtsələnd] 31
Japanese	[ˌdʒæpə'niːz] 37		Tanzania	[ˌtænzə'nɪə] 🔊 2.2
Kendall	['kendl] 🔊 1.22		Texas	['teksəs] 112
La Scala	[lə 'skɑːlə] 🔊 1.52		Thai	[taɪ] 🔊 1.24
Lake District	['leɪk dɪstrɪkt] 🔊 1.22		Turkey	['tɜːki] 🔊 2.2
Lima	['liːmə] 53		Turkish	['tɜːkɪʃ] 🔊 2.2
Lyon	['laɪən] 19		Vienna	[vi'enə] 162
Manchester	['mæntʃɪstə] 🔊 1.21		Wales	[weɪlz] 127
Maryland	['meərɪlənd] 🔊 2.5		Zurich	['zʊərɪk] 🔊 1.21